Some Helpful Tips For Prepping

AKA

SHTF Prepping

Donald Pontious

DEDICATION

I would like to dedicate this book to my grandparents and my mother.
May God be ever watchful over you.

CONTENTS

ACKNOWLEDGMENTS

I would like to acknowledge the people who have helped me over the years. Kieth & Cathy, Wayne & Cheryl, Dustin, Bruce & Debbie, Eric, and the rest of my extended prepping family, thank you. Without your feedback and advice, your criticism and praises, the tears and the laughter, much of what I learned would be untested and untried. I appreciate your patience. I would also like to acknowledge Amazon and their subsidiary company Createspace, without whom this book would never have made it to print.

CHAPTER 1
PREPPING, THE LARGEST GAME OF "WHAT IF" ANYONE CAN PLAY

Being prepared for disasters, and other life changing events really all boils down to playing "what if" with yourself.

Now, as strange as it sounds, if you have played the "what if" game, and played it well, you have examined every potential scenario. You have also thought of the things needed to address that scenario, hopefully well in advance. If you are like me, you look at the worst possible case scenario and play "what if". If you are prepared for the worst case scenario, then the lesser emergencies life throws at you will be easy to handle. A "cake walk". A "breeze", if you will.

For example: you are fully prepared for a hurricane knocking out the power, water, and other basic services for a month or more. A severe storm blows through and a tornado touches down, knocking out the power for a couple of weeks. You are easily able to handle the lack of water (water is pumped to your house using electricity), electric power, even telephone.

If you prepared for a long term outage (in our example a hurricane knocking things out for months) you easily have enough food, water, a way to cook, a way to heat your house (if there is cooler weather outside), light sources for night time, and plenty of basics (anything you may buy from a store from toilet paper to toothpaste) for just the couple of weeks that the power is out.

It also works in reverse. If you have followed the US Government's minimum guidelines for disaster preparedness (and only *those minimum guidelines, no more, no less*) you have enough food, and water for 3 days. What you do not have a way to cook that food (they make no such recommendations). They do however, (if you do enough research) recommend methods for cooking food, such as using your charcoal grill, chafing dishes, candle warmers, fondue pots (assuming they are the non-electric variety), even a fireplace (assuming you have a: wood and b: skill enough to cook over open flames).

Do you have a chafing dish and enough gelled alcohol fuel? A non-electric fondue pot and an adequate supply of gelled alcohol fuel? A fireplace and an adequate supply of wood? Heck, do you even own a grill, charcoal or gas, and do you have adequate fuel to last for weeks, if not months of multiple times a day use? These specific items are not addressed by our loving Government.

If you are following the Government guidelines, you will also have the following minimum of equipment, which I have listed in **bold**. My comments follow each item:

A battery powered or hand cranked radio, extra batteries for each. OK, how many batteries are enough extra batteries? They do not say.

A flashlight and extra batteries. Is *one* flashlight enough and how many extra batteries should you have?

A first aid kit. The first aid kit, an extremely important item. How extensive? What kind of injuries will the first aid kit treat? Does it have enough supplies - pain relievers, burn gels, triple antibiotic creme - in it to last at least for 3 days worth of treatment and wound care? How do you treat more severe injuries?

A whistle to signal for help. Good idea, especially if you get buried in rubble. You use less energy to blow a whistle than yell over and over again.

Dust mask(s) to help filter contaminated air and plastic sheeting and duct tape to assist with "shelter in place". OK, one of my biggest beefs with the US Government recommendations. A dust mask does exactly nothing against real dangerous contaminants. The same with duct tape and plastic sheeting. The only thing these really protect you against is *contaminated dust*. In the case of contaminated dust you need have several dust masks to swap used for new. They get clogged, and become useless.

Moist towelettes, garbage bags, and bag ties for personal sanitation. Really? I mean really? You are better off with keeping a large plastic garbage can - never used for anything - in your garage or in a spare closet. Use it to store your kids stuffed animals in. When you know you may lose your municipal water, pull it out, fill it with water while the water is still running. Use this water to fill and flush your toilet. Toilets are gravity flush operated. Just use a 2 quart pitcher to refill the tank from the garbage pail. *Always* remember the Florida "hurricane rule": if it's yellow let it mellow. If it is brown flush it down. You can also use the water from the garbage can to give yourself a sponge bath. Just fill your bathroom sink with some water, clean your important parts, and drain. Save the moist towelettes and the garbage bags for *if* the sewer system is backed up or backing up. You should have a "disaster toilet" for this case – a specially designed toilet seat that fits over a 5 gallon bucket - and some kitty liter on hand. You line the 5 gallon bucket with the garbage bag, toss a little kitty liter on the bottom, and place the toilet seat on top. After each use, sprinkle with a little kitty liter. This helps reduce the odor. When the bucket gets half full, remove the bag, seal it well, and place as far from your house as possible.

A wrench or pliers to turn off the utilities. If you do not know where the shut-off valves for your water and/or natural gas are, or how to operate them, you better learn now. The same can be said for electric. If the power goes out for any period of time, turn off the main breaker for your house or apartment. This will keep your expensive electronics and appliances from taking a surge when the electric service is restored. You will know the electric is restored when your neighbor's AC compressor kicks on, or street light come back on.

A manual can opener for food. Better yet, have 2. If one breaks or you lose or misplace one, you have a spare. They are cheap and worth their weight in gold when you have to open a can to feed yourself.

Local maps. These are actually handy. If there are trees blocking roadways, or bridges are washed out you need to know any alternate routes you can take to get to where you may be going.

Cell phone with chargers, inverter, or solar charger. I say all three. An inverter charger is one like you plug in to your car 12V power port also known as a cigarette lighter plug. No grid power and a regular charger is pretty worthless. A solar rig to charge your cell phones are not a bad idea, but you *must* understand they are limited and slow. It may take days to fully charge your cell phone. Days, plural. All of this is, of course, assuming that the cell phone towers are still operational -

they run on electricity too.

So you see, you would be pretty hard pressed to stretch 3 days of food and water out to a week, or even 2 weeks. You could very well be in dire straights by day 5.

Do you know the rule of 3's?

3 minutes without **air**

3 hours without **shelter**

3 days without **water**

3 weeks without **food**

3 months without **hope**.

Can you see where I am going with this? If you have the *minimum* recommended by the Government, you have exactly 3 days of water on hand for *one* person. Have you considered that people drink more when they are hot or performing even moderate physical labor?

You have to have water more than you have to have food. If the water systems are down in your area for 14 days, and you only have 3 days worth in your place of residence, how are you going to survive the other 11 days without water? You will not. It is really that simple.

The FEMA guidelines are a good place as any to start, but they are just a start. You are not prepared if you have just the basics. In the following chapters I will go into more detail about changing your lifestyle into a prepping lifestyle. It is easy, inexpensive, and not so intimidating as you may think.

Beginning Prepper Advice

A question was asked on one of the many preparedness boards I frequent by someone who is just starting to prepare:

"(I am) Looking for feedback on the percentage of money to be spent on priorities for prepping. I could spend all of my energy and money at the local firearms store but that's not practical, I like food so that's easy for me and I'll drink water if I have to. Would the percentage of time and money be a fluctuating subject or should it be a constant? The reason I ask this is that sometimes I feel that I'm ignoring one priority for another. I wish I could approach prepping more uniformly"

Here is what I answered: There is, in my opinion, no set hard and fast rule of percentages for prepping. I do it out of habit, and it is just part of the budget. For example, when shopping, if I buy 5 cans of vegetables, I grab 3 more for the shelf. If I buy a 5 pound bag of rice, I buy another for the shelf. Small steps make the biggest difference.

Spread your big purchases, like guns and ammo, for example, to times when the bills are paid and you have extra cash in the bank not accounted for. Start with the basics, water/food/protection.

There is an excellent beginner bulk food strategy for less than $300.00 that has the less than glamorous name of "Scotch Broth". There are enough calories and nutrition in this for a family of 4 for a year:

This is really easy recipe to change in countless ways. By adding left over meats or vegetables, even adding dried vegetables to the mix you could totally change it up. It wouldn't have to be the same old thing every day. This is what you will need :

4 x 22lb (or 10kg) rice. (Any kind will do – parboiled is the best compromise, it lasts almost as long as white rice and contains the B-12 vitamins everyone needs).

2 x 11lb (or 5kg) kidney beans

2 x 11lb (or 5kg) barley

2 x 11lb (or 5kg) lentils (yellow)

1 x 5.5lb (or 2.5kg) green split peas

1 x 5.5lb (or2.5 kg) chick peas (garbanzo beans)"

30 pounds of bouillon cubes (added to each batch as you cook it)

I recommend splitting the bullion between both chicken and beef bouillon. Bullion is added into the cost and it **is** reflected in the $300.

To assemble for storage:

Put two (2) bags of the rice in a mixing container (a food safe 5 gallon bucket). Then add each of the other ingredients 11 pounds (5kg) at a time, mixing as you go. Be sure to be wearing gloves or your hands will be shredded by the end of the mixing.

When you have all the other ingredients mixed in with the first two bags of rice, add the last two bags of rice and *really* mix well or you'll get all rice on the bottom of your mixture. You can leave it in the bucket or you can measure out 16 ounce potions and bag them in food saver bags.

Making the soup:

Take 16 ounces (by weight) of the dry mixture and add to 6-7 quarts of water. Adding a nut of butter or a tsp. of olive oil will help prevent the soup boiling over and add essential fats.

Add 3 tablespoons (or to taste) of powdered soup stock. Then add any veggies, meat, and seasonings you like.

Bring to a boil and let simmer for two hours and you have enough soup for two days for 4 people.

On the second day you'll need to add some more water (it thickens in the fridge overnight) and another tablespoon of stock. Make sure to boil for at least 10 minutes the second day to kill off any potential bacteria, - especially if you are not storing in fridge, but just in a root cellar or like that in the event of no electricity in summer.

Make your own bread and have a thick slice for dunking with a large bowl of this delicious soup and it serves as a main meal. You are *full* after just one (large size) bowl of this stuff.

Kids will usually only be able to eat half a bowl with bread, or a small bowl, whichever you prefer. Adults will likely want a nice big bowl.

If there is any mixture left on the third day, just add the new mixture to it.

This and some greens is all you need to exist, especially if you use "converted" rice, which contains vitamin B12.

Along with the basic recipe there are also other suggestions to make this truly an excellent source for your long term food storage. One thought that I had was that this would be a good way to have some "charitable" foods on hand.

If you were to do this over and over again across 12

pay-days, you would have a 10-year food supply in just under 6 months time.

It boils down to this: food for 4 for 1 year is food for 2 for 2 years, and food for 1 for 4 years, all without breaking the bank. Prepping does not have to cost an arm and a leg.

Caveat: I am a *frugal* prepper, always have been. We shop the 99cent Only, and Dollar stores for preps. Not necessarily food either. For example on the medical side you can buy, at the 99cent Only stores, 4 tubes of triple antibiotic ointment for the same cost of 1 tube from a "national" box store - whether that be grocery, drug, or other store.

Another tool that works to your advantage is Warehouse stores like Sams Club or Costco. No, not on the per-prepared or boxed foods, but on hygiene supplies and bulk food items like rice, beans, powdered milk, vacuum sealing supplies, etc.

In my area, Costco also has bulk Liquor – hard liquor - stores attached. Large containers of good quality grain alcohols, excellent for trade, or limited medicinal uses. Those same bulk stores are now carrying "survival" foods and some supplies.

Stay away from these pre-packaged "Survival Food" offerings! They are overpriced for what you get. You are better off building your own "buckets, bags, and boxes" of survival foods, equipment, and materials.

I acknowledge that the inflation is hitting hard so we continually take baby steps. I have been unemployed for one and a half years, and *still* manage to put away a little every time I go to the store.

Another thing you may want to look at your budget for is gardening. Consider putting in a garden now, when you do not need to rely on it, so you can gain experience, if you have to. This allows mistakes to be made that will not cost you food you may desperately need. Also focus on developing skills and getting the basic equipment for things like canning.

Within the past year I have gotten back into reloading ammunition and building hand loads because I acknowledge the fact that one day, perhaps very soon, ammunition will not be available in store or through "normal" venues, and replacing it would be problematic. I bought a little at a time and built my tooling and supplies up to where I can effectively load or reload my ammunition 1000 times per caliber I shoot. It took months, but was well worth it.

As with anything dealing with prepping it is a personal thing. This is what I suggest to lower the worry and impact on your time and budget. Build prepping habits and skill sets, this is not a hobby, this is a mindset and lifestyle.

Prepping as a Parent and Spouse

Recently I came across a blog post by a prepper who was speaking about how having a wife and children has affected the way he preps and lives. I thought perhaps I could expound upon this a little bit.

When (and if), in the course of our life, we get married, our lives change. If we are lucky, we will have a spouse that balances out our idiosyncrasies. If we are not, well, then we have a lot of work ahead.

I am single. I live a pretty spartan lifestyle. I did not have a lot of spare income, because I chose to spend it on things I wanted and live poor for a little while. When I was married that was very different. Suddenly, I was accountable to another person. Then came my son. Now I was not only accountable to another person, but then I had this defenseless human being relying on me to provide food, shelter, and protection.

If it were just two relatively healthy adults, pulling a "bug out" would be difficult enough. With a young child(or children) in tow, on foot, it will take a big horde of zombies or Mount Vesuvius erupting nearby to get us moving. So we had to fit our prepping to our needs. Not because we think bugging in is ideal, it is because bugging out would be extremely problematic, to say the least.

In a nutshell, you must look at your personal circumstances. You must choose the best path for

you and your family. If you are a single guy/gal prepper, a couple with no children at home, or a family with two adults and 3 kids, you will approach prepping in a different way.

If it was just my self and a partner, we would probably have a months worth of food - dehydrated or freeze dried. We would have packed a set of bug out bags, and a lower amount of other preps. We would be bugging out.

However, because of a child, we had had to readjust our focus. We have bug out bags, and if it gets bad - zombie horde or volcanic eruption for example - we would have done our best. My focus has always been on building a secure and adequate source of food & water, basic necessities, medical supplies, and security equipment.

Since I am no longer married, I am not "bugging-in" or sheltering in place, but that foes not mean I do not have to assess and judge my local area. I could be forced to shelter in place or bug in. I am aware of all potential additional water, food, and raw materials. Prepping is a complex and personal **mindset**. Prepping with children is even more complex and personal. Be prepared mentally as well as physically.

Chapter 2

The Survival Triangle

Part 1, The Base of the Triangle

"You shall be known as Usul, which is the strength of the base of the pillar." – Stilgar – Dune

Food and water should be the base of the survival triangle. Water should take priority over food, when you start getting prepared.

Water is the foundation of all life. The human body is comprised of 55-78% water, dependent on body type. Water, not money, is the lifeblood of civilization. Without it, a body and a civilization die.

"Never tell me the odds" – Han Solo – The Empire Strikes Back

One of the basic rules you learn in survival training is the "Rule of Threes":

3 minutes without air

3 hours without shelter

3 days without water

3 weeks without food

3 months without hope

After three days without water, you become dehydrated. Your heart and respiration rates begin to increase to compensate for decreased plasma volume and blood pressure, while body temperature will rise because of decreased sweating. At around 5% to 6% water loss from normal body functions (breathing, urinating, defecating, blinking), one may become groggy or sleepy, experience headaches or nausea, and may feel tingling in one's limbs (parethesia). With 10% to 15% fluid loss, your muscles become spastic, your skin begins to shrivel and wrinkle (decreased skin turgor), your vision dims, and urination will be greatly reduced, becoming painful. Delirium begins to set in. Losses greater than 15% are usually fatal. So you have decreasing odds of survival the longer you go without water.

"Water, water everywhere, Nor a drop to drink" – *The Rime of the Ancyent Marinere* – *S.T. Coleridge*

The human body needs water. A healthy human adult requires approximately 1 gallon of drinking water per day to survive. This should be the foundation of your preparedness triangle. The base. There are literally hundreds of ways to physically filter (Burkey, Britta, Pur), chemically sterilize (bleach, iodine), and physically sterilize (straining and boiling, sun sterilization, solar distillation) water.

This water requirement is for drinking only. I am not including sanitation or cooking. Double the amount for basic sponge baths and cooking needs. We are now up to 2 gallons of water per day for relatively comfortable survival.

Water can be collected from rain run-off, hot water heaters, surface sources, and if you are lucky wells.

Another source of water, especially if you home-can, is from canned vegetables. This water is chock full of water soluble vitamins and minerals that leech out of the vegetables you preserve. Just make sure to watch your salt usage when canning, especially if you are suffering from Hypertension (high blood pressure) now.

"I was thinking of the immortal words of Socrates who said, 'I drank what?'" – Chris Knight – Real Genius

You need a source of clean, potable (non-contaminated, drinkable) water. If you live in a city, water can be problematic when the power is down and the local pumping station is offline. The best thing to do – right now – is secure water for yourself and your family.

Get jugs, bottles, cans of seltzer (let it go completely flat and you have water), or even fill   barrels with water. Calculate how much water you will need for one month, at least, and get it stored.

In the event of an extreme emergency, you can fill your tubs for flushing your toilets – no drinking this- there may be soap or chemical residues that can kill you.

Always follow the Hurricane Rule of water conservation: if it is yellow, let it mellow. If it's brown, flush it down!

"Either get busy living, or get busy dying" – Ellis "Red" Redding – The Shawshank Redemption

When an event occurs that significantly affects the way you live on a day-to-day basis, any preparations you make today will keep you alive!

You may not live in the lap of luxury, but the alternative is far worse. You may perhaps survive long enough to weather the event's aftermath. You may not. Nothing in life is certain except death and taxes. Any lack of the base of the survival triangle, which is food and water, and you may as well use your time wisely, dig a grave and lay down in it. Deaths from starvation or dehydration are horrific.

Water After TEOTWAWKI

Now you understand about the importance of water as a preparation.

In this section, I will discuss a specific type of water treatment that is shelf stable, lightweight, and easy to use.

Calcium Hypochlorite - AKA pool shock. If you buy this, make sure you buy the full strength - 78% Chlorine - without algae preventive added.

You can get this at most pool supply stores or big box marts. This stuff is cheap, easy to handle, readily available, and easy to use, and not hazardous except to maybe stupid folks.

A 1 pound bag costs about $3.00, and treats (at full strength) *drumroll* approximately 12,000 gallons of pool water!. The up side is that it is a powder, and lasts forever. It weighs a pound, but you can get a 5 bag box from Wally World for about $12-$15. That is enough powdered chlorine to disinfect approximately 60,000 gallons of *pool* water.

It never goes bad or loses it's potency while it is in an unopened package. Liquid chlorine, on the other hand, eventually loses its effectiveness, as the dissolved Chlorine Dioxide (the main ingredient in liquid bleach) evaporates into a gaseous state. The fumes of liquid chlorine are explosive.

Additionally, a gallon jug of the stuff weighs 8 pounds. Not exactly easy to carry around with you. You should know that when liquid bleach is stored at 0-70 degrees Fahrenheit the shelf life is only 6 months. Every year after that it degrades in strength by 20% until all you are left with is salt and water. Meaning, it loses its potency over time.

Storing at temperatures much higher than 70 degrees Fahrenheit causes the bleach to lose its effectiveness and degrade more rapidly. However, for water sterilization, you require 6% sodium hypochlorite (full strength liquid bleach), you should change your supply of liquid chlorine every 3 months.

Calcium hypochlorite (powdered bleach) on the other hand is A: shelf stable, B: able to be mixed in small batches, C: is always at full strength since it is mixed directly as needed, and D: One pouch weighs 1 pound.

Using granular calcium hypochlorite to disinfect water is a two step process.

1: To make a stock of chlorine solution (do not drink this!) dissolve 1 heaping teaspoon (about one-quarter of an ounce) of granular calcium hypochlorite for each two gallons (eight liters) of water.

2: To disinfect water add one part of the chlorine solution

to 100 parts water to be treated. (1 gallon "bleach" disinfects 100 gallons water). Let the mixture sit for at least one-half hour before drinking.

There are 96 teaspoons (approximate) in one pound. That is 19,200 gallons of treated drinking water in one tiny pound of this stuff, since the dilution is different than *pool* use. Using it at the strengths for shocking a pool (full strength) would result in a dead survivalist.

I cannot stress this enough, do not use as directed on the package!

It should be noted that I treat the created bleach solution just like sodium hypochlorite (regular old liquid bleach), as far as shelf life goes. Replace your stock of bleach every 3 months. Better to be safe than sorry.

I also recommend you bring your water to a boil first, to kill the lively critters, and help settle the particulate. Let cool fully, strain or filter, then add the bleach solution you made (1:100 ratio - which is to say 3 tablespoons of bleach solution to one gallon of water).

One $12.00 box of this stuff (5 of the 1 pound bags) is enough to make 96,000 gallons of "bleach" treated water. That is a pretty sweet deal if you are in a place where you have access to water, don't have room for huge containers, and still want clean drinking water. Plus, you can take this with you if you have to bug-out or leave your bug out location. It is extremely portable and easy to use.

Additionally, I have prepared several "trade" bags. I put 1/2 pound of calcium hypochlorite in a ziplock, with laminated "direction for use" cards and then put in a vacuum bag and vacuum seal it closed.

What is it worth to someone to be able to disinfect water, clean their "tighty whiteys", bleach cloth diapers, sterilize bandage material, clean your cooking and eating utensils, and overall maintain a semblance of reasonable cleanliness?

To help dissipate the excess chlorine from treated water, you can also allow the treated water to sit in an open container for 24 hours.

If you fill a fish tank with straight tap water without adding a de-chlorination chemical, you can allow the water in the tank to sit for 24 hours and the chlorine levels will evaporate to "safe for fish" levels. Chlorine is very volatile.

If you have clear bottles and a good flat surface in full sunlight, you can use the UV radiation put out by the sun to purify your water, chemical free.

It seems that a standard 1 liter water bottle (clear and without a label), if left in direct sunlight for 6 hours, allows in enough UV radiation to "sterilize" the water in the bottle.

This is called the SODIS method and has been used with extremely good results in places like Africa.

Personally, I will probably do both the chlorine and SODIS method. Standard water purification plants use a combination of chlorine and UV to purify what comes out of your tap.

Keep On Eating In Lean Times

We are fast approaching, here in the United States, some definite turning points that can affect you profoundly.

One of those turning points is economic hardships coupled with increasing fuel costs. What does that mean to you, and I for that matter? Two words: food costs.

Food and fuel are directly tied together. Whether we like it or not, when the cost of transporting those canned goods, vegetables, meats, breads etc. goes up, the prices of those goods goes up as well.

You have a good job? Decent income? How good? How decent? Let me propose for you a basic scenario: a weekly budget for your house.

At current fuel pricing where I reside, it costs about $75.00 to fill the tank of my vehicle. I spend approximately $200.00 for food per week at current prices.

These two items alone can make, or break a family budget. Notice I am not including utilities or housing costs, just food and fuel.

Total for 1 week food & fuel: $275.00, at current pricing.

Fuel is $3.49 gallon today. Crude is at $100.00 a barrel for April delivery. That is 38% higher than 2 months ago.

Bump your fuel and food costs up just 15% more.

Fuel would be $4.01/gal

Fuel: $89.39/week

Food: $230.00/week

Total: $319.39, a difference of $44.39

Bump the fuel and food by 45% from this weeks pricing:

Fuel: $108.74

Food: $290.00

Total: $398.74 - nearly $400.00 a week, which is $1200.00 to $1600.00 per month!

You can see where I am going with this. Please, stay with me, this is extremely simplified to illustrate my point. Read on, intrepid one!

We are seeing something very subtle. The economic

structure of the US is under immense pressure. Rising fuel costs in a recession is a dangerous thing. There are ways to help mitigate the crushing costs and gain some economic freedom. Gardening and small livestock, most notably. It is about being prepared for a full on depression.

Here is a good example of an average suburbanite prepper family's ideal plan to feed their family when the stores are too expensive.

Please note, my grandparents grew up during the depression, so they taught me a lot:

#1: is eating/preserving what you can produce: garden (Square Foot Garden or container gardening for those facing square foot challenges), raise rabbits, goat for meat and milk, chickens, ducks for eggs and meat, etc.

This cuts down significantly on your reliance on grocery stores and cash on hand.

#2: Stored food. As you read previously, FEMA recommends that the average family have 3 days food/water on hand "just in case". If you truly want to be prepared, shoot for a minimum of 1 month. Best case scenario? 1-2 *years* of long term storage food.

One point I want to make is the food storage you *gain* out of gardens/small livestock. I am talking about drying, canning, etc. When you *get* a harvest, you cannot eat everything. You must learn to preserve that bounty in some way, thereby extending your (hopefully) already existing food storage.

So, that being said, buy the appropriate materials/books and learn how to can **now**. Not later, after you desperately need a way to preserve that bumper crop of squash, or that overabundance of tomatoes. Learn now while you have the leeway of being able to make mistakes, because in a survival scenario, your margin for error is very, very narrow, and quite possibly non-existent.

If you are not gardening and raising food animals (like rabbits, which can be raised *anywhere*, including an apartment more on that in the next section) right now, then you are setting yourself up for definite failure, should we have a severe economic crisis.

Besides, is there anything bad about lowering your bills and eating organically grown, home cooked food? I can't think of any, myself.

Another thing that is essential to preparing properly is: store food that you normally eat. If you decide your food stores for Hurricane season or that potential emergency needs a little beefing up, your best bet (as far as health, nutrition, cost, and ease of use) is storing food you already buy and eat on a regular basis.

That means no MRE's (Meals Ready to Eat), freeze

dried foods (unless you camp extensively and eat these regularly), or buckets of "emergency food".

Why?

Well, for one thing, you may not even like the "new" food's taste, smell, texture, or even how it looks (it may look plain gross to you). Also, there is a very significant cost and comfort factor involved.

Thirdly, there is the digestive issues to consider. All of these things are *doubly* important if you have kids.

Let us consider an an MRE - These military meals are highly concentrated, heavily vitamin fortified, and superlatively preserved. They pack a *huge* dose of calories, vitamins, and minerals all in one go.

However, the taste is not very good (due in part to the recipes that are used, and the heavy vitamin fortification), and they are *very* expensive (even the "cheap" MREs run about $7.50 per meal per person).

Also, the current MRE, according to regulations, should not be consumed as your only food source for more than 21 days straight (3 weeks), and I can personally attest to the ramifications of subsisting on them for 30 days with no supplemental foodstuffs as recommended, such as fruit and milk.

It was a gastrointestinal disaster – I hurt badly. The things one learns after a Hurricane devastates your residence are amazing.

The best thing for your preparations are some good old fashioned homey items like jerky, bullion cubes, granola bars, packets of crackers with peanut butter or cheese, boxes of animal crackers, Cracker Jacks, tea bags, instant coffee single serving tubes (about $1.00 for half a dozen at the dollar store - Taster's Choice - both leaded and unleaded varieties), various condiments and spice packets, graham crackers, flour tortillas, instant soup packets (Cup O Noodles for example) - all of which can be vacuum sealed and stashed in your preparation stash. The sky is the limit, use your imagination.

I even suggest buying items like "Soup Starter" or "Stew Starter" (try to find the ones that are just dried vegetables - no "soup bullion" etc.) and portioning it out into small vacuum bags. They make a great addition to plain bullion, add vegetables (nutrition, substance, texture, and taste), and make what would be just a cup of broth into a nice meal.

Bonus 30 minute bug out/camping meal recipe:

Beef jerky (the real stuff, not the moist junk you find in a Jack Links bag) cut or broken into chunks, dropped in pan of boiling water, add a beef flavored instant soup packet (like onion soup mix), pour in a small pack of your "Soup Starter" veggies into it and you have a very hearty soup with meat ready in 30 minutes.

Spices go a long way to making otherwise unpalatable, bland, or different foods more appealing. The weight is negligible and worth adding to your BOB (Bug Out Bag) or preparations, especially of you have children.

As for adding raw goods like flour, "and such" (like sugar, etc.) to the BOB, the weight to benefit ratio is exceeding small. Not knowing what others may intend to use flour, sugar, etc. (I consider salt a spice and necessary addition to a BOB) for, I can only say I am not carrying much in the way of raw goods.

Most of my BOB food is either prepacked, or requires little in the way of preparation and fuel to heat. All foodstuffs are hermetically sealed in bags, with all the original packaging intact.

Bug Out Bags (commonly called "BOBs") are not intended to be lived out of for excessively long times. If you are not within, say 3 days walking distance of where you are going to bug out to, you may want to consider altering your plan to include a lightweight all terrain "wagon" to tote your excess gear.

Otherwise, you need to research things like long distance, extended period hiking, such as the Appalachian Trail hikes, where hikers literally carry everything they need for weeks at a time on your back.

Items like freeze dried food, micro light camping and

hiking gear, as well as tips and tricks from experienced long distance hikers can go a long way towards preparing you for a longer duration or distance bug out.

Knowledge weighs as nothing and can be gotten for free off the internet with some diligent searching and research. It is worth the investment of time to learn these things.

When you are preparing for any contingency, you have to look at *all* contingencies, and again, play the "what if" game. Ask yourself things like "what if I have driven my vehicle halfway to my Bug Out Location and the vehicle is damaged or breaks beyond easy repair"?

Asking yourself a series of questions like this and trying to look at as many contingencies as possible will help you not only feel more prepared, but *be* more prepared.

In a crisis situation, the less energy you have to expend to solve problems, the more you have to spare for getting where you need to go or doing the things you need to do.

Be sure you do NOT store potent items like mints in with foods that absorb odors or flavors (like rice).

Prepping is about logical practicality, not gear. It is about being ready to ride out those emergencies that hit our life in comfort. This is not about "surviving", this is about thriving.

Stealth Livestock: An Expansion on Prepping in a Suburban Setting

Stealth livestock.

When you say those words it elicits images of cows wearing black SWAT uniforms or ninja goats. However, it is a lot simpler than that.

Livestock, no matter their size or type, produce 2 things in excess - noise and waste. The average suburbanite has noise restrictions and nuisance laws to deal with. Additionally, a suburban prepper needs to be mindful that his or her neighbors may become the marauding horde looking for food in a TEOTWAWKI scenario.

So how does a suburban prepper go about finding and implementing a livestock base that is both productive and easy to keep quietly?

First start with some research. Here are some things to look at:

Try and ascertain how much yard square footage you

have, and how much your potential livestock will need.

For example, large breed rabbits need about 3 square feet per animal. The up side is you can stack the cages one atop another (about as high as you can comfortably see in), as long as you have the right trays to catch waste between them.

So that means approximately 3 large breed rabbits would only take up three (3) square feet of yard, but use approximately 9 vertical feet of space.

Check the noise level generated by the potential livestock. Let us take a look at Muscovy ducks.

They are one of the heaviest of the duck breeds. They produce meat, feathers, and eggs. They are also quiet. The females (called ducks) never get louder than a quiet churl, and the males (called drakes) make a soft hissing.

So they do not quack, cluck, moo, bray, bleat, or crow. Winning!

Feeding. This one is mostly overlooked by the novice livestock keeper. We will not be able to buy feed from the feed store after a TEOTWAWKI scenario. We need to know what the animal can eat from forage, what we can grow to feed them, and what we need to know about their ideal diets.

Waste produced. This one is relative. You could have the quietest, most space efficient livestock, but their waste matter reeks to high heaven! In the above examples, rabbits and Muscovy ducks produce waste products that have little to no offensive odor as long as you clean up after them regularly.

I must reiterate - the most important thing is cleaning up the waste products efficiently and quickly. If you garden, I would strongly suggest making a compost pile and putting the waste materiel on it. This literally turns crap into food.

Once you have decided on the animal or animals, do not rush out and buy a whole load of them. You will need to buy good reference manuals on the animals. Preferably you will be able to find one that covers all aspects of the animal from selecting, housing, feeding, caring for (diseases and common ailments and their cures), and if it is a really good book - how to process the animal and recipes using what the animal produces.

Read this book. Build your animal housing. Acquire the basic equipment, then buy the animals you are set up for.

So far we have talked about Muscovy ducks and rabbits. Other quite productive yet quiet animals are: fresh water fish (research "backyard aqua culture") and bees (fresh honey, yum!).

If you have the space and less restrictive laws around you, you may even consider miniature goat breeds.

On a related note: If you have children, be sure that you have had the "these are not pets" discussion. Nothing will hurt your pocket book for preps more than a gaggle of animals that your kids will not eat!

You waste money on feed and time on caring for them. One way you can avoid any problems is name your breeding animals, but not the offspring.

For example, I named all of the breeding does and bucks in my rabbit run. Any kits (baby rabbits) born are not named at all.

In fact I processed all of the animals at home, and my belief is children should be exposed to this fact of life from an early age.

Another method of keeping the "pet" mentality out of the picture is minimal handling and petting of the animals, as well as minimal exposure to them. Being around the animals at feeding and watering time, handling them to check their general health (wing clipping, or checking to see if the animal is in season for example), handling them if you have to clean their enclosures, and handling them on the way to be processed.

No petting, no "just holding". This is business. These animals are a survival food source. Treat them like the investment they are. Care for them, but do not get too attached. You cash in on all of your investments, eventually.

If you have to replace a breeding animal, select the best of the best kit or kits, with qualities you are looking for in further offspring, and separate them from the rest after they are fully weaned. Name them and enter them into your breeding records. Breeding animals that can no longer produce should be relegated to the stew pot.

Waste not, want not.

Black Gold, and I don't Mean Oil

"Fertilizer does no good in a heap, but a little spread around works miracles all over." - Richard Brinsley Sheridan

One of the most important things a prepping gardener or small scale farmer can do is start composting.

Compost is natures fertilizer, and if you feed the pile correctly, you will have rich, black gold to reinvest in your garden that could very well yield the largest, richest crop of fruits and vegetables you have ever grown.

Let me offer you some simple advice , though. Do not go wasting your money on commercial "composting barrels" or "compost generators" even if you live in an apartment, you can compost on your balcony. All you need is the space for your compost and the knowledge of how composting works. I will cover composting on an apartment balcony in a later book.

For right now, let us say you are a homeowner and have a 3 foot by 3 foot section of yard you can dedicate to composting.

First things first - the containment unit. I have seen composting done in large plastic trashcans (with some serious modifications), in wire mesh enclosures, and open piles.

Let me say that you will have to decide what is right for your space, your budget and your time.

I built a partially enclosed, two section composting bin that only cost the time it took to pick up the materials and put them together. It is made from free pallets from Freecycle and held together with some 3 inch long deck screws.

Now you have the enclosure, what next?

Well, you should understand what compost is and what it is really used for. Composting creates a dark brown, crumbly material. Your garden loves compost for several reasons: it's full of food your plants desire, it's chemical-free, and helps the soil retain moisture.

Though it can take years for soil to rebuild lost nutrients on its own, amending the soil with compost speeds up that process.

A compost pile gets "fed" with two kinds of organic materials, green and brown. The brown materials provide carbon, an energy source to the bacteria and microorganisms who decompose the materials, while the green materials provide nitrogen.

Finding a balance between these two will improve the "heat" of your pile and prevent problems from occurring.

Green materials include items such as:

* plant matter from your garden

* green grass clippings

* pulled weeds

* green table waste, such as fruit and vegetable peelings (Cover food scraps with soil to prevent drawing pests.)

* coffee grounds and tea bags

Brown materials include things like:

* dead leaves

* dead, dry grass clippings

* plants that have wilted and gone brown

* pine needles

* twigs (shredded)

* sawdust (from wood that has not been chemically treated)

* shredded paper

Items that should not be used in a compost pile include:

* meat or bone scraps

* fish

* dog or cat waste (you should not use any manure from dogs, cats, or other meat-eating animals, since there is risk of parasites or disease organisms that can be transmitted to humans.)

* coal ash

* leaves from magnolia, oak, holly, black walnut, and poison ivy

* grease

Get your compost pile started using by layering the

materials. Compost piles should be started on bare ground, not on gravel or concrete, to improve air circulation and to allow microbes and organisms from the earth access to the pile.

First, create a 8 inch layer of organic materials, a mixture of your "greens" and "browns". Make sure that there are plenty of coarser materials included, like untreated wood chips, to ensure good air circulation

Next, add a thin layer of fertilizer. Animal manure (for example rabbit pellets on the pile) can be used, or you can use blood meal, 1 to 2 cups should do.

Every time you "feed the pile", make sure you add the blood meal or animal manure. If you use any animal manure other than rabbit, it **must** be composted before adding it to the garden.

Lightly water each layer as you go, and continue until you reach the top of your bin or run out of material.

Alright, you have gotten your compost pile started.

Now what?

The Care and Feeding of Compost Piles

As the new, proud owner of a compost pile, you have two options. You can either wait patiently for 3 to 4 months for your rewards (compost). This option is less labor-intensive, requiring that you turn the pile at 5 to 6 weeks and lightly water the pile.

Or, you can continue adding fresh material to your compost pile. This requires more frequent turning, and watering (we do this weekly). Though this method is more work, it makes more regular use of the scraps leftover from meals and yard work (for those who are composting for the benefits of recycling), and will produce an ongoing supply of compost.

Now, for a caveat: I live in Texas, and where I live my pile does not go dormant in the winter time. If *you* live in a place where the temperature drops below freezing for extended periods (more than a couple of days a year), your pile will go inactive in the winter months, unless special steps are taken. If you want your pile to remain active year round, please "Google" Winter Composting.

Part 2 The Left Leg of the Triangle

Where's the Heat? – The Essentials of Heat and

Shelter

"And now for something completely different" – Monty Python's Flying Circus

Up to this point, you have read about food & water, the basis for a preparedness triangle. Now we will explore an essential leg of that triangle – shelter and fire.

What was a caveman without a cave and fire?

Extinct.

Shelter is rather self-explanatory. Shelter keeps the elements off of you. It is the only barrier between you and the outside world.

Without intact shelter, you will eventually succumb to extremes in weather. Without shelter, you are completely exposed to the other "elements" which may seek to harm you or your family – the criminal element.

Lets face it – in an economic collapse, crime will run rampant before full out societal collapse occurs. So shelter is important for more than keeping the rain off of your head.

Ideally, shelter is not a 4 season tent out in the boondocks. It is your home. A place both comfortable and familiar, a defensible place that keeps you and your family dry, safe, and warm.

"Oh, my liver is killing me..." – Prometheus

Fire is the second most important element, after water. Without fire, we have no civilization. Without fire we have no electricity. Without fire we have no industry. Without fire, we freeze in the winter, possibly to death, eat raw food, andsome foods if left uncooked are poisonous.

Fire is heat, light, and life. While you could technically survive for some time without fire, the comfort level will be exceptionally low. Fire gives comfort. This book I am writing address being prepared so you live in a level of comfort beyond "survival" and hopefully into "thriving".

"Gimme fuel, gimme fire, gimme that which I desire" - Metallica "Fuel"

Fire needs three things fuel, oxygen, and spark. Fuel can be as simple as cut wood and as complex as LPG systems. If you live in an "all electric" home, propane heaters and camp stoves are (currently) inexpensive. However, you need fuel no matter your heat/cooking source. In an economic collapse, you would need enough fuel on hand to feasibly last you a full year.

Much like Argentina, when the economy collapses, the infrastructure remains, but utilities such as electricity are sporadic and unreliable at best. This means you should have enough fuel to cook food and heat your home for one full year without electricity.

Another thing to consider, if you have the space and wish to be as prepared as possible, is providing yourself with multiple ways to heat your home and cook food. A fireplace, propane or kerosene heaters, and propane or multi-fuel stove would be a good selection to have.

Some even serve two purposes. You can heat your home and cook with a fireplace. Some kerosene heaters are stoves as well. Select and prepare with a variety of methods to ensure you will not go without when you need it most.

An additional consideration to make – do you have adequate, safe storage for whatever fuel you will need? Some homeowners associations have some very strict rules on how much firewood you can store or how much propane you can have on your property. Safe storage of fuels, especially the volatile ones, is an extremely important consideration to make.

One last note – from a safety aspect: ***never, ever burn charcoal briquettes in an indoor fireplace***. They are loaded with chemicals and give off huge amounts of carbon monoxide that may not vent out of your home properly and could kill you and your loved ones.

"Come on baby light my fire" – The Doors "Light My Fire"

Spark – the second component of fire. Matches, lighters, magnesium fire starter sticks, fire pistons. All devices used to create sparks and flames.

Make sure you have at least three different ways to make fire, and enough of each to last a year. I have lighters, matches, and magnesium fires starter sticks on stock at my house – enough of each one to last nearly a year each. That is a years worth of matches, flints, and lighter fluid.

Learn to light a fire without a match. Last winter I lit every single fire with a magnesium fire starter stick. It was a challenge and by winters end, I felt fairly confident if I had nothing else except the starter stick I could not eat cold food or be cold.

Being reliant on ignition systems and piezoelectric starters found in most propane systems is fine, until they stop working. The wires erode, they fall off. The ceramic breaks, a hundred different things can happen to that spark generator.

For example, most older (pre-1970's 1980's) natural gas stoves used a pilot light to light the stove top burners. The more modern stoves have an electric ignition system (that "snapsnapsnap" you hear when lighting your gas stove is an electrical spark arcing through the stream of natural gas). When the power goes off, you best have a way to light that stove or you have a big problem on your hands.

"Chestnuts roasting on an open fire" – Torme and Wells "The Christmas Song"

The image of a roaring fire and the sound of the fire crackling bring forth memories of comfort and family. Once, the home was based around the hearth, because that was the center of the home. It was where the home was heated from and where the food was prepared. It may soon be the same way again.

We are headed for a very serious economic reckoning and if you are not ready for it, you and your family may be victims of the economic perils rather than the survivors. The next leg of the preparedness triangle is security.

Without any of these things: water/food, shelter/heat, or security, you will be a victim.

Part 3, The Right Leg of the Triangle

The Essentials of Security

"An armed society is a polite society." – Robert A. Heinlein "Beyond This Horizon"

The last leg of the preparedness triangle is that of security. Security is a complex and manifold idea, at the core of which is the firearm.

Here in the United States, we have, ostensibly, the easiest society in which a private citizen can legally own a firearm. Various pacifistic elements of society, along with your very own government wish to take that key of personal defense from you.

Post Hurricane Katrina is a prime example of illegal gun seizures that left citizens defenseless in the face of violent criminals.

The worst of these instances was when an elderly woman was threatened, harassed and physically attacked by Police officers when she refused to give up her revolver – her only means of defense in post Katrina New Orleans.

Since the widely publicized occurrences of illegal firearm seizures by military and police personnel, many

states (Alaska, Florida, Idaho, Kentucky, Louisiana, Michigan, Mississippi, New Hampshire, Oklahoma, South Carolina, Virginia, and West Virginia, Texas, and Arizona) have enacted strict bans forbidding the police from seizing privately owned firearms in an emergency situation.

Sure. OK. This way lies the conundrum: who watches the watchmen?

What this boils down to is you absolutely must have some way to protect your food, water, shelter, and fuel from scavenging packs of lawless scum.

Don't think it'll get that bad? Have we forgotten the Rodney King riots, post Hurricane Andrew Miami, and Post Hurricane Katrina New Orleans?

"This is my BOOM stick" – Ash "Army of Darkness"

Lets start with the basics, shall we? The easiest, most affordable beginner home defense platform is a shotgun. Particularly the 12-gauge pump shotgun. There are home defense shotguns for as little as around $200.00, not including tax.

Shotgun ammunition is cheap and easy to get. Ladies, I recommend #4 buckshot loads in your shotgun. The recoil is easily manageable, there is very little secondary wall penetration, and it is still lethal.

Nothing says "Don't Tread On Me" like the sound of shotgun slide being racked in a dark room.

No matter what your preference, be sure you have a way to defend yourself, your family and your stuff!

"This is my rifle, this is my gun. This is for fighting, this is for fun." – Full Metal Jacket

While owning a firearm (or firearms) is an important first step, nothing, and I repeat nothing beats skill with that firearm. Boston T Party, in his excellent book "Boston's Gun Bible" pounds home the lessons you should learn.

Lesson number one: use money to turn bullets into skill.

It is better to have bought 1000 rounds, shot 900 of

those rounds and have 100 rounds left than having bought 1000 rounds and never fired a single shot.

Frankly, a person with zero skill and a ton of ammunition is just being kind to the criminals and animals in his immediate environs.

Lesson number two: Become a rifleman!

Allow me to elaborate, a pistol and a shotgun have their uses…like getting you to your rifle. Nothing beats a large bore rifle in the role of a defensive weapon.

"A gun is a tool, Marion, no better or no worse than any other tool, an axe, a shovel or anything. A gun is as good or as bad as the man using it. Remember that." – Shane

We need to hold the gun up and examine it as a tool. Like any good tool, it has multi-purpose applications. From self-defense, to hunting, a good weapon is only as good, or bad as the person using it.

Taking one of the myriads of training and education classes out there is a must. Even an experienced shooter benefits from these classes.

If you are an "experienced" shooter and you just scoffed at that statement, I pray you never have to guard my back. You will get yourself and very likely someone else very dead, very fast.

Train. Train often. Train hard. Focus on accuracy, discipline, and control. If you can afford it, take a tactical handgun course and a tactical rifle course. At the minimum, train with friends who have the same mind set as you. Going to the rifle range is fine, and good fun, but it is *not* training.

"I like to keep this around for close encounters." - Corporal Dwayne Hicks - Aliens

Regardless of what weapon you choose, keep it close, keep it ready, and keep it safe. Your life and the life of others will depend on the reliable accurate and controlled use of that weapon.

It is imperative that you understand that securing yourself takes more than a deadbolt and a dog. If you are a pacifist and don't believe in guns, can you at least have the decency to dig a grave in your yard before the economy collapses? It'll make it easier to handle your remains after the strong arms come through and loot your place and kill you.

I will not die on my knees. Will you?

Chapter 3
Thinking Outside of the Box

We all do it. We fall into patterns, both in our lives and our thoughts. We get so accustomed to doing things one way, every time. The same can be said of our perceptions and our thoughts.

We should, when we have time in our lives, sit back and contemplate everything we think, everything we do, and all of our perceptions. What do I mean?

Allow me to make an example and explain.

Joe Public is the average work day man. He rises at the same time, 6:00 AM (give or take a few hits on the snooze bar) and gets dressed for his day. He wanders to his kitchen where he starts the coffee pot, then he wanders out the front door and gets his daily paper. He sits down, starts reading the paper- the front section- but it is like white noise to his brain, nothing really sticks.

When the coffee finishes, he pours himself a cup and continues reading the paper, now he is in the sports section, his attention perks up and his brain engages. He sees game stats, player names, stadium names, reads about the latest rumors in the sport, and notes when his favorite team will be playing next, and these details he will ***not*** ***forget***.

Why? they are extremely important to him, they entertain him and do not cause him unease or frustration.

Let me stop here, and make a caveat. I know I am being deliberately generic and perhaps downplaying the importance Joe Public places on the headlines. Then again, how many people do *you* personally know that read the paper on a daily basis? I mean *really* read it? I personally know **one**. That is it.

The vast majority flip on the tube, catch a little morning news, or perhaps turn on their laptops and peruse the headlines at their favorite website.

Many do not. Many are on their My Face/Spacebook/Tweetle accounts within 30 minutes of rising. Many could care less about the news. More people place a higher importance on celebrity gossip or sports news than *anything else.*

Pretty sad.

Anyhow, you can see where I am going with the pattern thing. Being inside a box. Our thoughts get that way also. We become rigid in our thinking. We become so accustomed to the the way we think things are, that we cease to question and simply defend our stances, regardless of right or wrong. We also become complacent sometimes even apathetic.

Part of being prepared for the worst is thinking and

acting outside the box. Being active in our daily perceptions of the world around us, not just accepting or apathetic. Our thinking must be flexible as new rope. Our daily routine must be anything but routine.

This will allow us to not only be more aware of the things going on around us, but also be better mentally prepared to cope with sudden or catastrophic changes around us.

Your mindset is as much a preparation as storage food or guns and ammo. You remember the rule of threes?

1. 3 minutes without breathing (drowning, asphyxiation)

2. 3 hours without shelter in an extreme environment (exposure)

3. 3 days without water (dehydration)

4. 3 weeks without food (starvation)

5. 3 months without hope (depression)

Well, hope comes from inside. If you have a flexible mindset, you never will lose hope. There is always a solution, you just have to find it.

In one of my blog posts, I posted a scenario where a man asked his brother-in law to be a simple question: "What would you do in a society where you could not even afford a loaf of bread to eat?" The answer?

"Well, I guess I would just kill myself. I mean who wants to live in a world like that?"

The operable words here are **who wants to live?** I sure do, and I have adjusted the way I think, act, and even perceive the world. It has done wonders for me. Now instead of insurmountable obstacles, I see opportunities to do things differently. Can you say the same?

I Reject Your Reality and Substitute My Own!

There are times, in my life and when speaking to other preppers, I sense a deep frustration. They want so badly to awaken the people around them to the realities that we are all facing. They are at a loss.

In all honesty, sometimes I am too. It is very difficult to fight past normalcy bias.

Normalcy bias can and has resulted in unnecessary and additional deaths during extreme crisis situations. We, as a nation and as citizens of the world, are being faced with the grand-daddy of all economic collapse scenarios. I need not go into all the nasty details. If you read my with any regularity, or even are a new reader, just review my past posts.

People are literally experiencing overload. They know on an instinctive level that something is not right. This is where the normalcy bias kicks in. Normalcy bias is also known as the "sheep effect".

Studies have shown that in natural disasters, like hurricanes, that more than 70% of people check with others before deciding to evacuate. This causes significant issues with planning for disasters. The normalcy bias also causes people to drastically underestimate the effects of the disaster.

Therefore, they think that everything will be all right, while information from the radio, television, or neighbors gives them reason to believe there is a risk. This creates a cognitive dissonance that they then must work to eliminate.

Some manage to eliminate it by refusing to believe new warnings coming in and refusing to evacuate (maintaining the normalcy bias), while others eliminate the dissonance by escaping the danger.

The lack of preparation for disasters often leads to inadequate shelter, supplies, and evacuation plans. Even when all these things are in place, individuals with a normalcy bias often refuse to leave their homes.

This is what we are fighting. All I can tell you is do not give up. Eventually you will get them to reject their reality and substitute your awakened reality.

Do not lose heart.

Crying Wolf?

"The tree of liberty must be refreshed from time to time with the blood of patriots and tyrants. It is it's natural manure" - Thomas Jefferson

I have written about TEOTWAWKI, and the possible economic collapse. Knowing what I am thinking about may help you get focused on the problem at hand.

The other day I was thinking about the boy who cried wolf. Remember that endearing tale?

Anyhow, I was thinking about the upcoming announcements of the Federal Reserve Chairman, Ben Bernake and the following day, President Obama will make another speech regarding his "new jobs plan".

OK Enough with the crying wolf already. There is inflation and there are no new lasting jobs the government can create.

Getting a real and honest politician would be a refreshing change. Oh, wait. I am talking about politicians. Speaking of...can any of you remember when an "Elder Statesman" was someone to be looked up to?

I cannot, myself. However, the image remains, and that image *came from somewhere.*

Gone are the days of the nominally honest politico. Gone too are the days when a congressman's and senators tenure was measured in terms, not decades. Complacency and laziness have caused our downfall.

We are the only ones who are to blame for the current state of affairs.

*We, **the people,*** are ultimately the employers of the very politicians who have destroyed our country out of greed and personal gain. We should have cut off the paychecks, reduced the benefits package and hired a whole new staff, but we did not and it is our fault.

I have done my fair share of fist shaking at the powers that be. Admittedly it is out of frustration and the feeling of powerlessness one gets when nothing changes no matter what efforts one goes to.

Oh, and please don't talk to me about the "Tea Party Victory" there was in 2010.

These so-called fiscal conservatives turned chicken and balked when the money ran out. Can't have that. So they create this bogus bill that has $2 Trillion in tax cuts over 10 years and hikes the national deficit, which had already doubled in the former 1.5 years, by another $2.6 Trillion. Net savings? Negative 10% per year, average. That is the interest the United States must pay the Federal Reserve on the loan of the $2.6 Trillion.

You see, we borrow our own money from the Federal

Reserve Bank; actually we borrow permission to print our money from them, for a fee (interest) of course. The rub is we already owe the interest on the existing debt.

Where does the Federal Government get the interest to pay off the loan? That is the kicker: it was never created in the first place, so the taxpayer has to pay more and more in taxes to meet the fiscal shortfall. As it stands the US has nearly $14.7 Trillion in debt, not including $65 Trillion in **unfunded** liabilities.

What? Oh, let me explain that one.

An **unfunded** liability means the US Government has promised to pay or is obligated to pay (liability) some person, organization, or other government.

The unfunded part? Well, that means is we just don't have the funds to pay the liabilities.

No moolah. No dinero. No jeng. No ching-a-linga-ling. Broke. Flat busted. You get the picture. It gets even better.

Former Federal Reserve Chairman Alan Greenspan stated recently, specifically, and openly that "The US Will never default, we can print all the money we need to".

Yeah, "we" could. When that happens, we drop into a

hyperinflationary spiral that will kill this country so fast we'll be wiping our butts with cash because it is cheaper than toilet paper. See how nasty this gets? Wait! It gets even better!

Now we have Asia, particularly China, who is the second largest holders of US Treasury Bonds (the first largest holder? The Federal Reserve Bank).

What is the issue with this? Easy. When China buys Treasury Bonds, it does so with Remimbi or Yuan. Which reeduces the money supply in China, making China look poorer, and America gains X $, making America look richer.

Temporarily.

Understand that these bonds have a percentage yield. Remember US Savings Bonds? Treasury Bonds are just massively big ones. They state that they will yield a certain percentage in gain when they mature.

Where does the gain come from? Yes, you guessed it, the taxpayer's pocket. Well, not yet anyhow, and here is why: when the bonds have matured over all these years, the foreign investors, like the Chinese government has opted to "roll" or reinvest the yield of those bonds in new bonds. So we have not had to pay up in full yet. Notice, I said yct.

So in recent times, China sees that so much of their own money is tied up in the US dollar. They have explosive exponential growth that is almost out of control. Matter of fact their national interest rate is currently over 6%, and they are talking about raising it. They have also stated very implicitly that unless the US changes it's fiscal policy they will have no choice but to withdraw their fiscal support to protect their currency and economy.

What does that mean? Simply put, they sell the Treasury Bonds back to the US before they mature fully. They lose the interest they were "making" but they also re-infuse their economy with a large (approximately $1.2 Trillion) liquidity injection.

Oh and the US would owe China that $1.2 Trillion dollars. Immediately. On demand. So the Treasury would have to borrow $1.2 Trillion from the Federal Reserve Bank (as discussed above), adding the new money to our $14.6 Trillion Deficit, *not including interest*.

The secondary effect of a massive sell off of US Treasury Bonds by China? All other foreign countries who hold our bonds would follow suit, seeing the Chinese move as a vote of "no confidence" in the US's credit.

The Treasury borrows from the Fed, and the money is added to our deficit, *not including the interest* we would owe on that money, and the America we know and love dies, not a noble and glorious demise, but a death by a thousand cuts.

So I continuously rail at the powers that be, saying "quit "crying wolf" with Afghanistan, Syria, Libya, and Iraq." I beg people to quit blaming Bush. Step up and fix this.

A good start would be by repealing the Federal Reserve Act of 1913, then abrogating all debt incurred under this system and replace our current currency with a true representative one (gold standard, based only on how much gold the US actually owns.

It is a finite amount and therefore only a finite amount of money can be printed) or the American people - when they really start understanding these things I have written about - will step forward and decide it is time to "refresh the Tree of Liberty".

China, Precious Metals, and the World

OK bear with me, this will be rather involved but worth knowing. To understand China and precious metals, you must understand a culture that is literally thousands of years old.

Notice, I said culture, not government. Political systems come and go, but the basic culture is relatively unchanged.

To understand, in this case, precious metals and China, you must understand first and foremost that precious metals have been, worldwide, currency for literally thousands of years.

"Gold is the money of Kings, silver the money of gentlemen, barter the money of peasants, and debt the money of slaves."

This saying has held true and holds true to this day. Going back to the first real contact between China and Europeans, not the intermediary of the Silk Road (but the Silk Road plays a part in this), you find that in the late 1400's into the early to mid-1500's the discovery of the New World and the wealth it contained. The Spanish (and by default the then subject country of Portugal) jealously guarded the routes to the riches of the New World and Far east.

Fernando Magellan discovers the Pass of Magellan in 1520, making stabs westward into the Pacific possible. This shortened the travel from Europe into Asia. It allowed Spanish settlements in South America, supported and driven by the Church, to expand into the exotic Far East.

This move was driven by greed and power. Now, China and Japan had contact for centuries. Each had something the other wanted, but because of a state of open hostility between the Japanese and the Chinese, trade was limited at best.

The Chinese wanted silver. The Japanese wanted silks. Enter the Spanish.

Because the Muslims had a choke hold on the Silk Road, and therefore all trade with Asia and China, Christoper Columbus made his voyage in 1492. While it was not the only reason for Columbus's voyage, it played a part in the decision made to finance it.

The Spanish discovered the New World, and jumped off westward across the Pacific Ocean.

They made contact with both China and Japan and arranged to become neutral intermediaries for trade, for a fee of course. Spain grew richer, as did China, and Japan.

The use of silver ingots (taels) for currency in China can be traced back to 206 BC, the beginning of the Han Dynasty.

Even though during the Soong Dynasty, the Chinese became the first country in known history to issue paper currency, *trade was still done in silver*. Paper currency fell to the wayside, only to be revisited in the Ming Dynasty from 1368 to 1450.

It was discontinued due to rampant inflation.

Now, in China, large and small trade transactions have always, since the first portion of their recorded civilization, been performed in taels of silver.

The accepted Imperial Treasury Standard weight of a tael was the Kùpíng Tael - 1.27 troy ounces of silver.

The common everyday money was a copper alloy called (translated into) Copper Cash. This was the everyday currency used for gambling, minor purchases, etc. Significant and large transactions and trades were always performed in taels of silver. Always.

Silver has represented wealth and currency for over 2000 years in China. It is only after the Peoples Republic of China (PRC) was formed, and the ownership of gold or silver was made illegal that this stopped. The PRC made it illegal for Chinese citizens to buy, own, or hold silver or gold for only 50 years. 50 years.

Now, the PRC encourages the people to buy gold and silver, and they have gone precious metals crazy!

They have a thousands of year old culture centered around wealth, power from wealth, and the accumulation of wealth that has only been suppressed for about 50 years.

In 1950, China had next to nothing in gold reserves. Today they rank 10th in the world. That is only the government holdings being counted, that is not counting privately held bullion.

In 2012, the government of China banned silver from being exported. By July of 2012, it was being promoted as an "investment" to the Chinese public on the 6 o'clock news.

You do the math. How does it affect global demand for gold and silver if just 10% of Chinese begin to perceive precious metals as an investment?

From what I'm seeing from the financial reports I read, the Chinese government is engaging in one of the most explosive financial marketing campaigns in history. Instead of Maoist propaganda, though, they are attempting to reengage the Chinese public in the gold/silver markets.

Simply put, the Chinese has triggered a national gold and silver craze.

The Chinese public now has gold trading platforms on steroids. If you are Chinese, you can buy silver bullion or gold bars at any Chinese bank in four different sizes. Wealth management products tied to gold are skyrocketing in popularity, and the public can now instantly buy, sell, and trade gold 24 hours a day in five different forms with different eight types of services.

Also, for the first time in history, Chinese investors can even trade gold abroad (in London) with the swipe of a "Lucky Gold" card.

What about China's food supply, you ask? Oh, so you do understand that they import a lot of food, tonnes of it, annually.

Good question, but moot. When the world fiat system implodes, Gold and Silver will *be* the currency used to buy and/or sell oil, food, services, goods, etc. When you hold massive wealth ahead of the collapse, the collapse itself looks less threatening. Besides which, with their infrastructure taking a minor hit when fiats implode, they will be standing ready to buy food from whomever needs to sell it.

The BRICs countries: Brazil, Russia, India, and China already have unilateral trade agreements in place. Brazil produces and exports tonnes of beef, soybeans, wood and wood products, fish, petrochemicals, steel, automobiles, aircraft, and consumer durables that account for nearly 36% of their GDP. That is just Brazil.

Combine that with the exports from India and Russia, and you have demand met by supply. All China does is change their Chinese made goods into export from China to Brazil, India, and Russia, and any other country who wants cheap manufactured goods for precious metals, food, oil, or whatever.

Losing the US import/Export market would not hurt China as badly as most folks think. The PRC has known about and been planning for the collapse of the fiat system for 50 years.

Their hand may have been forced a little with the collapsing of the US and EU economies, but not by much. Right now they are playing economic games trying to buy some extra time, but it is completely a hurry up and stockpile kind of maneuver.

They are not desperate, they are just really wanting to have their "larder" a little fuller. Like any good prepper, they know they need more of what they have, but could muddle through if they have to.

China is rabidly encouraging and expanding governmental and public gold and silver consumption in preparation for a massive crash of the worldwide fiat systems. The handwriting on the wall is exceptionally clear. The financial world as we know it is about to implode upon itself.

China will come out smelling less like poo and more like a rose, with massive precious metals backed wealth to hold onto world superpower status. Mark my words. I may be wrong. Hell, I pray fervently that I am wrong, but the signs are abundantly clear to me.

Chapter 4

Practical Skills and Why You Need Them, or

Knowledge Weighs Nothing

The New Normal

What will the new "normal" be after a massive TEOTWAWKI/SHTF event? Well, if you are like me, you play the "what if" game. What if...it is the worst possible outcome it could possibly be?

Imagine, if you will, after struggling for 6 months to maintain a semblance or relatively "normal" pre-collapse life, you are now unable to generate or maintain regular power generation.

Your stored food supplies are dwindling faster than you calculated, because you are feeding an extra 4 people you did not prep for (your brother and his family). You have no livestock, no idea how to get any, and no idea even how to feed them. You have a seed bank but have no clue what to plant, when to plant it or in what quantity.

Your alkaline batteries are about gone, and you have no way to charge your re-chargeable batteries.

Your stored water is running out, and while you have a lot of surface water nearby in a large pond, you are uncertain if the water is chemically contaminated, requiring purification methods that you do not have.

You sit in your kitchen, staring out the window, worried.

You thought you had approached prepping the right way. You bought all the right stuff. All the best gear. You read all the blogs, forums, and newsletters you could find. You read every post-apocalyptic collapse novel you could get your hands on a hundred times. You thought you had a great handle on things. What went wrong?

What went wrong indeed? You are not really prepared if all you do is buy food, batteries, gear, and books. You are only truly prepared if, and I mean *if*, you have cultivated, built and practiced a solid skill set.

A skill set is the one thing money cannot buy, but money helps. Skills are learned. Trial and error, experience, and mentors are the way to go.

Skills like gardening, land management, animal husbandry, woodworking, food preservation, and metal working for example. For me, I focus on skills that we (as a people) would have to know if we were living in the

1800's.

I cannot stress enough how important skills are. Without skills, all the gear in the world is just a waste of money.

Allow me to present you with a thought provoking fact: in the years leading up to the Great Depression, fully 90% of Americans were self sufficient and could grow and harvest adequate food for sustaining themselves and their families.

This number includes the 27% of the populace that were "farmers". Only 10% of the populace all of which lived in urban areas were not self sufficient.

Today, perhaps 1% is self sufficient - completely self reliant upon what they produce to feed themselves and their family. 99%+ of Americans are completely dependent upon others to feed them.

The die off after a TEOTWAWKI event is going to be massive.

Let me give you one example: electricity. Less than 30 years prior to my birth, electricity was not even commonly available in all areas of the nation.

My grandparents were raised and lived a good portion of their lives without electric power. My great grandparents lived without it for their entire existence. So did every other ancestor of mine.

The skills that we, the modern Americans, have sacrificed in the name of "labor savings", creature comforts, entertainment, and convenience, has enslaved us all to the grid.

If you are "off grid", unless you are living without power 100%, you have only substituted one supplier - municipal power - for another - yourself. You are truly not self sufficient unless and until you, me, and everyone else can live without electricity completely for any extended length of time.

I am currently making plans to cut the electrical umbilical cord and go for it. If anyone cares there is an excellent book I have been reading that deals specifically with just this subject...true independence. *True* off grid.

Humanity has existed for millennium. We existed without electricity, gasoline, petroleum products, and to some extent external threat over our existence. Sure, there has been slavery and oppression in the world. In every case until the advent of electrical power, you could see your oppressors with your own eyes. You could feel the chains on your wrists. You were able in some way to identify those people as your masters.

I am not a Luddite. I like electricity. Heck, I and writing this book on a laptop and it is being published electronically. I am not advocating destroying anything, I am trying to provoke some thought here.

You, every one of you, including myself, are literal slaves to electricity. Whether you generate your own power using generators, solar panels, water power, or draw from the grid, the majority of us could not live without electricity.

Living is more than the internet, computers, a cell phone, telephone, television, air conditioning, or washing machines. It is more than refrigeration, hair driers, DVD players, and coffee makers.

Living is so much more than these things, and we all fail at truly living, especially me.

When the electrical rates go up, and they will go up, your enslavement continues. At this point in our technological society every one of the people out there on the grid, even just off the grid, but generating their own power for use, are caught in the web inextricably.

You see, when electricity is super expensive, what do you think that does to the pricing of things like consumer goods, food, electronics, and clothing? Retail outlets will have to raise prices accordingly, as will manufacturers of raw materials, manufacturing goods, and finished goods. Anyone left needing these items is done for, financially.

True freedom is eschewing the very things that enslave you. Cast out the devices that keep you in your 72 degree womb. Comfortable in your air conditioned home, on the internet, watching your favorite movies, or even washing your clothes in a machine.

Making Soap The Old Fashioned Way Part 1:

Lye From Ash

A SAFETY DISCLAIMER AND WARNINGS WILL BE FOUND AT THE END OF THIS PART AND EVERY PAR PERTAINING TO SOAP MAKING.

Making soap is part chemistry and part art-form. The basics of soap are very easy to understand. Soap has three base ingredients:

Water (the softer the better)

Lye

Fat

Our grand parents, and great grandparents and so on all the way back into the dim and misty usually made their own soap. They did not have all of conveniences of society that we take for granted, for the most part.

Sure they had general stores or merchantiles and could get some "store bought" things, but soap was usually made by hand at the home.

Why? It was made from things that were on-hand, and with the right skills and some basic equipment, you did not have to buy anything.

What is lye? Lye is a corrosive alkali substance,

commonly sodium hydroxide (Red Devil Lye is Sodium Hydroxide), or potassium hydroxide (this substance can be leeched from hardwood ash, and was for centuries). It chemically reacts with the fats in a process known as "saponification".

There is a long, drawn out highly technical, scientific explanation as to what saponification is, but that is unimportant for this part. What is important is that you can acquire the basic ingredients from local sources and "waste" products of everyday living.

In this first part I would like to outline how you can make your own lye water from hardwood ashes. It is imperative you use hardwoods, because the potassium hydroxide you get from the soft woods like pine will only produce soft soap.

To begin the process you need a few basic pieces of equipment:

A water-tight bucket - a 5 gallon plastic bucket

would suffice

A drill

Fine gravel – regular, washed gardening gravel will work

Straw

White hardwood ashes (burn the hardwood in a really hot fire to produce white ash)

Soft water - collected rainwater is the best, it has no chemicals or dissolved minerals in it - you can use distilled water if you like.

2 cinder blocks

A non-reactive plastic catch basin

Chemically resistant rubber gloves and eye protection

A non-reactive storage container (plastic) for your lye water (I use a 5 gallon bucket with a lid, commonly available at your local hardware store).

Step-by-step instructions:

1: Drill small holes in the bottom center of the bucket - approximately 10-15 holes, in a pattern no bigger than the opening of your catch basin.

2: Put a 1/2" - 1" deep layer of gravel in the bottom of the bucket. layer approximately 2" of straw on top of the gravel. This is your filter media. It keeps the ash in and lets the lye water seep out.

3: Fill the bucket to within 2" of the top with white ash, it is important to not overfill the bucket, because the ash will float out when you start adding water. Pack it down gently, not too tight or the water will take forever to seep through, too loose and the water will not draw enough lye from the ash.

4: Take your catch basin and fill it to within 1-2" of the top with distilled or rain water. Slowly pour this into the ash, taking care to not overfill, again the ash will float out and it is a nasty mess to clean. Pour in stages if you have to. If you have packed the ash in your bucket correctly, the water takes a long time to seep through, so you have time to slip your catch basin underneath.

5: Set your ash bucket on the two cinder blocks (being careful not to block the weep holes) and slide your catch basin underneath. It takes a long time for all of the water to seep out so you can leave this for the day, come back tomorrow. Make sure no children or animals will get near the buckets as this is EXTREMELY CORROSIVE and HARMFUL. It will BURN unprotected skin. IF you get lye water on your skin - spray the affected area with Ammonia, the ammonia neutralizes the lye and stops the chemical from burning you.

6: Take your collected brown lye water and pour over the ashes again. Allow this to seep through a second time. When the brown lye water stops coming out, test it for strength.

To test your lye water for strength you can float a fresh (in the shell) egg or potato in it (wearing gloves and eye protection). If the egg or potato float about 1/2 way into the water - it is the right strength for making soap - remove the egg or potato and destroy them. Also, you can drop a chicken feather in, if the feather begins to dissolve, you have the right strength.

If the egg or potato doesn't float or the feather does not dissolve, you can strengthen the lye solution by boiling it down, much like making a reduction. Put the lye water into a non-reactive vessel (a stainless steel pot). NOTE: once you put lye water in the pot you can never, ever use the pot for anything else.

There is no way to guarantee that all of the lye is washed out and lye is POISONOUS. Boil the lye water down until it has lost about a third (1/3) of it's volume.

Let cool and test the strength again. If it is correct, then allow to cool and pour carefully back into the collection basin, and lid for storage. MARK IT CLEARLY - "LYE WATER - POISON – CAUSTIC".

DISCLAIMER: THE SOAP MAKING PROCESS INVOLVES A VERY CAUSTIC AND POTENTIALLY HARMFUL CHEMICAL - SODIUM HYDROXIDE OR POTASSIUM HYDROXIDE - COMMONLY KNOWN AS LYE. LYE IS A HIGHLY CORROSIVE HYGROSCOPIC SALT THAT WILL CAUSE ORGANIC SUBSTANCES LIKE SKIN, HAIR, AND CLOTHING TO DISSOLVE. THE INFORMATION LISTED HEREIN IS FOR EDUCATIONAL PURPOSES ONLY. USE PROPER SAFETY PRECAUTIONS - CHEMICALLY RESISTANT RUBBER GLOVES AND EYE PROTECTION WHEN HANDLING LYE. KEEP A SPRAY BOTTLE OF UNDILUTED AMMONIA ON HAND. IF YOU GET LIQUID OR DRY LYE ON YOUR SKIN SPRAY THE AFFECTED AREA WITH AMMONIA IMMEDIATELY! THIS WILL NEUTRALIZE THE LYE. THOROUGHLY WASH ALL TOOLS AND EQUIPMENT USED TO MAKE SOAP AND USE IT FOR NOTHING ELSE.

Making Soap The Old Fashioned Way Part 2:

The Fats

SAFETY PRECAUTIONS AND DISCLAIMERS ARE FOUND AT THE END OF THIS PART.

All right, now you have lye water, now what?

Well you need fat. Yes, fat, AKA oil, AKA grease. A good thing to remember about fats for soap making is:

The harder the fat is at room temperature, the harder your soap will be in the end.

Traditionally, animal fats were used for soap making. In the Ozarks around the turn of the century, people would collect their bacon fat drippings, boil them with water until they were "clean" and use that for making soap.

The soap had a smokey bacon-y smell - many guys I know would LOVE that- to smell like a strip of bacon. Others used the fat from beef kidneys – (suet).

This is a reasonably hard fat , most good butchers have it on hand, and it is almost pure right out of the animal.

All one needs to do is render the fat down. If you don't know how to render the fat, there are several good sources on the internet that take you through step by step but it is basically:

Chop the fat into 1/2" cubes

Cook over medium heat until all of the oils have been forced out, leaving you brownish bits.

Scoop the brownish bits out, place on paper towels, salt liberally and munch on these later (YUMMY).

Take the rendered fat and pour into a clean metal or high heat glass container and allow to cool to room temperature.

Additionally if you can get commercially prepared lard (rendered pork fat) from the grocery store, this is a good source of already clean, white fat. It is, however, relatively soft.

You should also consider any left-over fats from cooking - like bacon drippings – which can be collected, cleaned, and used to make soap.

There are several very good vegetable sources of fat available to us today: coconut oil, palm oil, cocoa butter (you can buy blocks of food grade cocoa butter on ebay), olive oil, etc.

Regardless of the type of fat this is the second most important portion of the soap making process. It is the chemical reaction between the fat and the lye that makes soap - saponification. The quantities of fat to lye will be addressed in the next part - Making Soap.

DISCLAIMER: THE SOAP MAKING PROCESS INVOLVES A VERY CAUSTIC AND POTENTIALLY HARMFUL CHEMICAL - SODIUM HYDROXIDE OR POTASSIUM HYDROXIDE - COMMONLY KNOWN AS LYE. LYE IS A HIGHLY CORROSIVE HYGROSCOPIC SALT THAT WILL CAUSE ORGANIC SUBSTANCES LIKE SKIN, HAIR, AND CLOTHING TO DISSOLVE. THE INFORMATION LISTED HEREIN IS FOR EDUCATIONAL PURPOSES ONLY. USE PROPER SAFETY PRECAUTIONS - CHEMICALLY RESISTANT RUBBER GLOVES AND EYE PROTECTION WHEN HANDLING LYE. KEEP A SPRAY BOTTLE OF PURE UNDILUTED AMMONIA ON HAND. IF YOU GET LIQUID OR DRY LYE ON YOUR SKIN SPRAY THE AFFECTED AREA WITH AMMONIA IMMEDIATELY! THIS WILL NEUTRALIZE THE LYE. THOROUGHLY WASH ALL TOOLS AND EQUIPMENT USED TO MAKE SOAP AND USE IT FOR NOTHING ELSE.

Making Soap The Old Fashioned Way Part 3:

Making Soap

Making soap can be messy and potentially dangerous. You will be handling some harsh, caustic chemicals and hot fats. ***YOU MUST TAKE SOME SAFETY PRECAUTIONS AHEAD OF TIME***.

It is **IMPERATIVE** you use safety goggles and chemically resistant rubber gloves.

Any and all equipment you will use for making soap will forever be for soap making only! Once you make soap with this equipment, clean it thoroughly and set it aside for future batches.

Once you have your safety equipment, you will also need:

1 Glass measuring cup

1 wood stirring spoons,

1 glass candy (fry) thermometers

1 large enameled iron or stainless steel 15 quart pot

1 old blanket (preferably wool)

1 kitchen food scale

saran wrap

1 plastic or wooden box for a mold

As far as ingredients, there aren't very many:

You will need, by **weight** (not liquid measure, they are *different)* a total of 32 oz. of Fats.

Caustics:

12 fluid oz of lye water

OPTIONAL: Lemongrass or other essential oil – 2 Tbsp.

Step by step instructions:

Take your wooden or plastic box (make sure it is large enough to hold your batch of soap) and line it with saran wrap. Set aside, this is your mold and the saran wrap is a release agent. It is not essential to have it, just nice. If you do not have saran wrap, you can pour the soap into the mold and cut it out with a sharp knife after it has initially cured.

Measure the lye water into the glass measuring cup. BE CAREFUL LYE WATER IS A CAUSTIC! - set aside.

Using the kitchen food scale, weigh your fats and place them into the pot. Melt the fat completely over medium heat and then pull off of the heat and let cool to 100-125 degrees.

Monitor the temperature closely. Once the fats have gotten to 100-125 degrees, slowly pour in the lye water, stirring constantly. Be careful not to splash while combining the mixtures.

AGAIN: BE CAUTIOUS - LYE WATER IS A

CAUSTIC

Stir until the mixture traces. Tracing looks like a slightly thickened custard, not instant pudding but a cooked custard. It will support a drop, or your stir marks for several seconds. If tracing takes more than 15 minutes, which it often does, stir for the first 15 minutes, then stir for 5 minutes at 15 minute intervals.

Once tracing occurs, add the lemongrass or other essential oils, stir to incorporate the oil completely. Make sure it is completely worked into the soap and immediately pour into your mold.

Cover the mold with the wool blanket and set it in a cool, dark place to cure for a few (2-3) days.

After 2-3 days check the soap, if the surface is firm, you can turn it out of the mold and slice it into bars for further curing. If it is not firmed up, cover and let cure until the surface is firm.

Once you have un-molded your block of soap, cut into bars and let cure and dry completely (about 2 weeks).

Once the bars are cured, wrap in saran wrap or waxed paper. This will preserve the fragrance and keep the soap from getting powdery residue on the outside.

This soap can be used to wash your body, your dishes, your hair, your clothes.

It costs pennies to the pound, especially if you make your own lye water, use recycled fats, and have some or most of the equipment on hand. The largest investment will be your equipment. This is defrayed, however by the cost savings across the board you will realize by making your own soap.

Hand-made soap makes an excellent birthday or holiday gift.

There are many, many books, websites, and videos on the web that detail soap making and it's many different aspects. There are specialty companies that sell soap molds, scents, colors, specialty additives, etc. Experiment. Have fun.

Above all, learn how o do this for yourself. It is one more step away from dependence on a grocery store for the basics. Also, these **skills** will be indispensable in a post- TEOTWAWKI scenario.

DISCLAIMER: THE SOAP MAKING PROCESS INVOLVES A VERY CAUSTIC AND POTENTIALLY HARMFUL CHEMICAL - SODIUM HYDROXIDE OR POTASSIUM HYDROXIDE - COMMONLY KNOWN AS LYE. LYE IS A HIGHLY CORROSIVE HYGROSCOPIC SALT THAT WILL CAUSE ORGANIC SUBSTANCES LIKE SKIN, HAIR, AND CLOTHING TO DISSOLVE. THE INFORMATION LISTED HEREIN IS FOR EDUCATIONAL PURPOSES ONLY. USE PROPER SAFETY PRECAUTIONS - CHEMICALLY RESISTANT RUBBER GLOVES AND EYE PROTECTION WHEN HANDLING LYE. KEEP A SPRAY BOTTLE OF PURE UNDILUTED AMMONIA ON HAND. IF YOU GET LIQUID OR DRY LYE ON YOUR SKIN SPRAY THE AFFECTED AREA WITH AMMONIA IMMEDIATELY! THIS WILL NEUTRALIZE THE LYE. THOROUGHLY WASH ALL TOOLS AND EQUIPMENT USED TO MAKE SOAP AND USE IT FOR NOTHING ELSE.

And God said "Let there be light"...

I have spoken before about fuel for heat and cooking. The byproduct of an open fire is light.

What about lighting the rest of your domicile in a TEOTWAWKI/SHTF scenario?

Camping lanterns are commonly propane or battery powered. So unless you have an infinite store of propane (and mantles) or batteries (and extra bulbs), you will eventually need a light source.

Hurricane lanterns, while extremely efficient, still require oil, wicks, and replacement chimneys (I have broken my share and a hurricane lantern without a chimney is worthless). You can rig up expedient oil lamps, also known as "tallow candles". However, you can also pour candles.

Cheaply. Now.

How? Allow me to illustrate.

A friend of mine is a teacher, and has, over the years, accumulated what seems like a ton of broken and used crayons.

A majority of these are made from soy wax (with a

colorant added). These can be a ready source of literally "free" wax, as they are for me.

Save this paper you peel from the crayons, it makes an excellent addition to home made "wax cup" fire starter/tinder (paper egg cartons with each depression stuffed with lint, paper and/or pencil shavings. Melted wax is poured into each cup, adding more lint, shredded paper, or pencil shavings, as needed to make sure the cup is full, and allowed to solidify.

Cut each cup out and you have a waterproof, highly transportable fire starting fuel. Just break chunks off with a knife, set in your tinder and light).

Another source of "free" wax is the leftover wax from previously burned candles. the stubs of tapers, the wax clinging to the inside of that big glass candle on your mantle that has no more wick, emergency candle stubs. Even those "scented wax disks" that you get for use in a scent diffuser can be used for a wax source. I like adding these to melting candle wax for a nice scent. Just be sure not to mix scents and you are golden.

The wax you are "scavenging" will not make pristine, white candles, unless you use only white crayons. While you can make "single color" candles, is it really worth it?

The color of a mixed crayon candle will be muddy and dark, but who cares? You are not selling these, they are for home use only. It is not like you are too worried about your decor in a SHTF scenario. Besides who really looks at the color of a candle?

Wicks can be made by soaking cotton string in a borax, salt, & water solution, and the very wax you are melting for candles.

Making regular cotton candle wicks is simple.

You'll just need some salt, borax, water, candle wax, and cotton string, yarn, or twine. You can usually find borax in the laundry detergent aisle of your grocery store. Some people use it to make their own laundry soap. You can vary the width of the string you use to make your wick in order to get wicks of different diameters.

1. You'll need to make a solution to dip the string in to make it into a wick. Mix 2 tablespoons of regular table salt, with 4 tablespoons of borax, and then dissolve that mixture in 1 ½ cups of warm water.

2. Drop a string into the mixture and leave it there for 15 minutes. If you're not sure how much string to use, measure your candle mold and add about 3 inches to your measurement. That's how long you'll want your wick to be.

3 .Pull the string out of the mixture and hang it up to dry. A clothesline and clothespins work perfectly for this.

4. After the wick is completely dry, melt some wax in a

double boiler and dip the wick into it. Make sure the wick is completely saturated with wax before you take it out. You'll need to use either a pair of tweezers or a paper clip to dip the wick into the wax so you don't burn yourself.

5. Pull the wick out of the melted wax and give the wax a few moments to cool enough so you can safely touch the wick. Then grab both ends of the wick and pull it tight.

6. Lay the primed wick out flat on a piece of wax paper to dry. Make sure it's stretched out when you lay it down so you'll have a nice straight wick when it's time to put it into a candle.

Using two hands, you can hold the wick (or wicks if you have a mind to make multi-wick candles) upright in your candle "container" as you pour the melted wax in. If you make the wick slightly longer than you need, you can tie a loop for holding the wick when you are pouring wax into the candle container, slip a pencil, pen, or chopstick through the loop and rest it on the lip of the container.

Cotton string - like "butchers twine" can be bought for $3.00 for 185 feet. If you reuse small Christmas tins, old (GLASS) jelly jars, you have reduced you cost down even further.

Heck, any heat proof container, like old, previously used glass candle containers, canning jars, even tin cans can be used as a candle container. I have made "milk carton" candles using old paper "quart sized" milk or half and half cartons to make some very nice square "pillar" candles as well. Just cut the top off, pour the wax (with the wick in place).

Once it cools completely, just peel the paper container off the candle.

Sure, I'm cheap, but saving money on stuff like candles, even cutting my cost down by a $1.00 each, is one more dollar I can spend on other preps.

Chapter 5
The Golden Horde?

A discussion about the civilian militias of history on a forum I frequent, turned as it usually does to a discussion of the after effects of a TEOTWAWKI/SHTF scenario. In this case the "Golden Horde" of J.W. Rawles prediction; the mass exodus of hungry, desperate city dwellers out into the rural areas seeking farms, and thereby food.

Think of the Wiemar Republic after WWI. If you know nothing of the farms and the fate of the farmers, do yourself a favor and research it. Read about it. Educate yourself.

The post got me to thinking...how will the exodus from the cities play out? This is something that is discussed among my friends and I on a regular basis. My friends are all former military (tactics and manpower specialist), current LEO, or current Federal officers.

There is not a lack of intelligence in this group. A lot of thought and deliberation over several years has gone into this. In a SHTF/Economic Collapse/WROL (Without Rule Of Law) scenario - (not inclusive of an EMP/Grid down or pandemic panic scenario), there will not be tens of thousands leaving the cities, at least not at first.

Even when they leave. It will not happen all at once, unless a massively nasty occurrence like a firestorm or hurricane drives them out. No single person is going to want to leave the security and safety of their "home" until the food runs out, and even then not right away.

They will literally not leave until there is no food. They will leave if there is no water and no way of getting it. Some will even stay until they are on the brink of starvation, thinking "The government will drop food", "They will send FEMA", "The Red Cross is coming" thoughts along those lines. Normalcy bias, its a real pain, and in this case *it will cost lives*.

I am going to state some very concerning facts right here: there are, according to the FBI National Gang Threat Assessment of 2011 fully 1.4 million active gang members in 30,000 total gangs in the United States - a 40% increase since 2009.

Active.

As in currently following gang activities etc. The number of "inactive" is higher still. That recent FBI document listed a startling fact: these gangs are recruiting out of and joining every single branch of the armed forces.

However, I digress.

Deaths from a serious TEOTWAWKI/SHTF scenario will be upwards of 75-80% of any population, the elderly, the critically ill, the ones who must have daily dialysis, those reliant on medications. I have discussed this before on many forums, and on multiple occasions with my like-minded friends.

Let us say within 1 month, 70-80% of the populace, is dead, from what ails them or lack of life saving medical help.

Add in attrition - murders, falls, infected cuts, lack of potable water, disease going untreated or under treated, fires, people dying of heat stroke (summer) or freezing to death (winter), animal bites (unfed dogs going feral, and attacking in packs), take another 5-15% off of the total populace of any given major city. That is anywhere from 75%-95% of any major metropolitan area's populace dead within one solid month of a massive SHTF scenario. If the SHTF scenario is an EMP or solar event, and the city is one like Los Angeles that must have almost all of it's water pumped in from over the mountains, advance the time line.

There will be, in my opinion and the opinion of others I know, 3 waves of exodus from the cities.

1st wave - lets call them the smart ones. The 1%. However, they are going to be leaving in dribs and drabs. Not all at once, and not all will take the same route. They will almost all, to a person, stick to major arteries of travel and not wander more than 1-2 miles off the highway. this exodus will last maybe a week before the slime balls get smart. The earliest ones out have the best chance. It will be small groups and families, say no more than 10 folks at a time. No real threat there.

2nd wave - Lets call these the awakening sheep – 1 week, perhaps 1 and a half weeks after the event(s). Food is not available, the water is shut off. They are sick and weak from lack of food, lack of potable water.

Many will not make it out of the city because the smart animals, the real low lives, will be set up on major roadways killing and looting the fleeing folks indiscriminately.

These animals will also be roving gangs of looters, snatching what they want by force, killing any who stand in their way. These are the hard core urban gangs, the organized criminal packs of animals that within hours of a SHTF will have "liberated" several warehouse/dock areas/food distribution centers.

I know of 5 within a 5 minute drive of my old house

and they are in "the bad part of town" where shootings and arson are common, nightly news occurrences.

The animals with military training or recruited folks out of the military...they know where the military keeps its supplies and armaments. They may also have military trained personnel in their ranks right now.

The people that actually make it out in the second wave will be the lucky, frightened, near starving, most likely sick ones that crept out on not so commonly traveled routes. Lets be nice and say 1% make it out. Scattered across a wide area, not much threat there.

Last (3rd) wave - This will be the worst. This will contain the real bad element that sees the handwriting on the wall.

Corpses piling up in the streets, disease running rampant, supplies running low, sewage backing up into living spaces, intermittent block to block warfare between rival "gangs".

Based on best case scenario calculations, 1 to 2 months after a SHTF scenario, the "Golden Horde" heads out. These are going to have their own problems (loose organization, fuel needs, water needs, food needs), they will very likely stay on the major arteries of travel (man is a curious animal, 99.9% of the time, they take the path of least resistance, even if going a different route will shave their travel time in **half**).

If they are smart send scouts out 2-3 miles off the highway to find fuel, food, supplies that the first couple of waves or other survivors may have missed.

These are the ones small towns and rural settlements on major roadways, and perhaps secondary roadways, will fear and have the worst time with.

Chapter 6

Bring Out Your Dead

There is one unavoidable, immutable statistic affects us all. 10 out of 10 people die.

In a total collapse SHTF scenario, how will you handle the dead?

I was asked a question about this matter not too long ago. I thought I would bring the discussion here and let you make your own decisions, and have your own discussions on the matter.

Question:

Not the most pleasant question but it is going to be a problem. Have you considered the stench of those unfortunate ones who did not prep and any possible solutions to this problem? I have been thinking how my neighbor and myself would deal with this. Do you have any suggestions?

My answer:

The stench is the least of your worries. There is one thing that must be addressed head on. Disease. Handling your own dead is one thing. Handling the masses of dead people after a major SHTF event when the die-offs end is a whole different game.

Approaching a corpse, even a long dead one (days, weeks, or even perhaps a few months dead), carries many risk factors. The least of which is the "gag" factor. Disease and rotting flesh go hand in hand. Besides the odor, you have insect vectors, airborne contaminant vectors, and animal vectors/issues (scavenging packs of once domesticated, now feral dogs comes to mind, as do wild scavengers). All of these things have to be looked at.

Additionally, a human typically voids their bowels when they die, adding to the disease issues. Just walking through an area with corpses can stir up airborne vectors you cannot see or smell.

You will typically have no idea how a person died, be that starvation, dehydration, disease, violence (including suicide), or natural causes.

Clean up of corpses after a major disaster like the Japanese Tsunami or even the Haitian Earthquake were handled with utmost care, and clean up crews wore personal protective equipment that ranged from just masks and gloves to full on sealed suits with independent air supplies.

Mass graves are a good way to handle a large number of corpses. Bear in mind, heavy equipment operation is noisy, and requires some skill (that could attract unwanted attention).

Burning the domicile down, is a 100% way to ensure no contamination (no corpses being handled and fire kills all disease vectors). However burning also throws a huge beacon into the air – smoke. Dark black smoke. The smell of a fire lingers for weeks afterward. It also would destroy any potential food or most any other scavenge-able goods in the structure.

Another question to ask - when lighting a fire - can we control this blaze? What happens if the grass surrounding the building is dry, or the woods the building sit in are dry, and they catch fire from a stray spark, and the next thing you know your BOL is under threat of fire, a fire you started?

My personal circle has very well understood protocols. All corpses are disease ridden. No exceptions except perhaps our own "group" members. Handle with gloves and a mask (even our "group" members) at the minimum, if at all.

We will not venture from our BOL for at the minimum of 6 months after a SHTF scenario.

That gives time for disease vectors to cycle, clear the area, and reduces our risk of accidental exposure. We will say a prayer over the dead, and most likely leave them where they lie.

Sounds cold, perhaps crass, but it is practical.

We cannot consume our time disposing of the dead except and only if they pose a direct threat to our group/locales hygiene/sanitation.

Dealing with your own dead is much different than cleaning corpses out of the suburbs. Your own dead should be washed, wrapped in a sheet and buried 5-600 yards from your water supply, at a minimum.

A pine box coffin would be nice, yes. Again, time, materials, and effort. Cleaning up the corpse of aggressors after you defend your home – in my opinion they are food for the wild animals.

Load them in a wagon or truck haul them off to an isolated area, mile, maybe a mile to mile and a half away, and dump them. Burial or cremation is too much effort for those who wanted you and yours dead. Hogs, buzzards, and coyotes have got to eat too.

Hauling dead animals away, or even corpses of attackers/undesirables consumes less time, effort and thought. Handle your own the way your morals and religious beliefs lead you.

If you are blessed enough to be in a smallish town, corpse disposal would then be a community discussion and effort that would very likely not take away needed manpower from other essential tasks for survival. Then mass burial, or even individual burial may not be out of the question.

My advice? If you are in a major city or a major city suburb and have to bug-in there, please consider alternative locations well away from the city or suburbs for a time (6 months to a year) after a TEOTWAWKI/SHTF scenario. If you need to return to your origination point for any reason, care and caution are   the   watchwords.

Chapter 7

Man Portable Power Options for Communications or Other Uses

Here are some options for "man portable" communications – specifically long distance communications, like a HAM radio. Bear in mind, this came from a discussion regarding the near infamous Chinese hand cranked surplus generator.

After much research, I have determined that setup will **not work** as it stands, and would need to be heavily modified, as it only outputs 6.3V DC. You need 12V DC.

An electrical engineer has posted some modifications on the internet, if you or your group is bound and determined to buy a hand cranked generator, you can look them up yourself.

All information is based on some basic math and knowledge of the systems being discussed. I try to give easy to understand breakdowns.

Using a pair of 7 amp hour (7aH) gel cell batteries (similar to the ones used in alarm systems, and uninterrupted power supplies). This is exceptionally portable, and if you throw in a solar panel with charging attachments, silent and literally free energy.

Note: the radio (or electrical gizmo) needs power pole connectors for the battery pack. You add some weight with the gel cells, but it gives you more transmit/reception time. The 7aH batteries are really cheap as well (about $20.00 each).

However, research has shown that a 12v 1.5w 120mA output solar panel from Harbor Freight which, while it runs under $20.00 requires about 66 hours of good daylight to charge one 7 aH battery to full.

Based on extensive research, I provide the following options.

Always remember "Fast, good, or cheap", pick 2.

Option 1: "Good and cheap"

At under $100.00 you can run portable, with extremely light weight.

Pros: Extremely portable (panel is 13.75"x4.75"x0.5"). Free energy from the sun (no labor needed), can charge the batteries while on the move.

Cons: exceptionally slow charging speed. Cannot run a small radio directly from the panel. Break down as follows:

1.5 Watt Solar Panel

1.5 Watt Solar Panel: $12.99 (trickle charges a battery. Will fully charge [from 0 charge to full] a 7 aH in approximately 66 hours under full sun -1.5 watt/12 V = approx .112 Amps. 7 aH/.112 A = 66 hours In direct sunlight.)

Connector wire set: $8.99

2 Qty. 7mA hour Gel Cell Batteries: $40.00

Total cost, minus tax or shipping: $60.00

Option 2: "Fast and good"

Allows for faster charging, more flexibility and a bit more cost. For just over $120.00 you can have a larger portable solar panel (14 Watt) that charges faster, and it comes with a connector wire set.

Pros: Extremely portable. Free energy from the sun (no labor needed), can charge the batteries while on the move.

Charges the battery in 1/10 the time of the smaller, lower powered cell. Can potentially run the radio (as long as transmission power is in the 4-5 AMP range, you are golden, as the radio draws less than the 14 Watt output of he panel) without any battery source during daylight hours. At 9 and 15 AMP TX you would drain a battery fully in .75 and .5 hours of constant transmission (approximate).

Cons: Larger solar cells (20"x15"x1.5"). Higher price point.

Break down as follows:

Briefcase Solar Panel: $79.99 (trickle charges a battery. Will fully charge [from 0 charge to full] a 7 aH in approximately 6 hours under full sun – 14 Watt/12 V = 1.1666 Amps. 7 aH/1.1666 amps = 6 hours In direct sunlight.)

2 Qty 7mA hour Gel Cell Batteries $40.00

Total cost, minus tax or shipping: $119.99

Please note, these charging times are very conservative as all panel ratings are calculated using winter time sunlight. Sunny locations with more daytime hours will give higher Amps, thus shorter charge times. One of the heftier 14 Watt portable panels will fully charge a standard car battery (40 aH) in 34 hours.

Also to note, the larger panel can be used to charge NiCads, relatively quickly with an adapter and battery charger hooked in (I have one that is cigarette lighter adaptable, and the large panel comes with a 12V DC "cigarette lighter female adapter"), or a separate charger can be bought.

I took the time and built two of the option #2. I housed the batteries in surplus ammo cans (water tight and nearly indestructible) and connected the batteries in parallel, thereby doubling the amp hours of the bank, while maintaining the Voltage (14 aH at 12vDC as opposed to 7 aH at 24vDC).

I lined the bottom of the ammo cans with 1/2" thick Styrofoam. I installed 6" tall 3/4" dowels as "legs" in each corner of the box, and installed a cover plate of 1/8" balsa ply with a power switch. I screwed through the outside of the ammo can into the legs to anchor them tight into the structure.

Sealing them with silicone, I painted them olive drab to match the outside of the can.

The foam and dowels keep the batteries tight in the box, yet keep an airspace around the batteries to help keep them cooler during use and charging.

The switch (which is recessed approximately 1/2" below the ammo can lid) allows me to turn the power on or off as I need. I ran a female "cigarette lighter" 12vDC connector with a cover cap to the outside of the box (sealing around the wire with silicone), wired to this to a charge controller (mounted under the wooden plate), switch, and then batteries.

My briefcase solar panel can be plugged directly into the batteries using the male 12vDC connector. any 12vDC item can be plugged into the system. If you know what kind of amperage your equipment draws, you can easily figure out how long you can run on this battery pack.

This was designed as a portable power pack for communications, but it can have many uses.

Chapter 8

IFAK on a Budget

One of the many things I have been working on for my preparations, for both camping and emergencies, is a very direct take on the IFAK or "Individual First Aid Kit". I know the practical purposes behind them and agree wholeheartedly that each person should have a medical kit of some sort on or about their person when camping or during an emergency.

What I cannot stomach is the high price of the commercially available IFAK kits available on the market - $120.00 to $229.00 for a pretty comprehensive Basic Life Support IFAK.

I also cannot stand the fact that many of them only resemble an IFAK in the most broad sense of the term "first   aid   kit".

So I did some research. The content list of an IFAK is readily available. Each and every item in a IFAK is available online through very reputable sources. Setting out armed with some knowledge and some time on my hands, I began to build my version of the IFAK on a budget. I added some items not necessarily on the list because I could afford to, and for practical purposes.

I need to add here that a vast majority of the items for the PEAK (Personal Enhanced Aid Kit) as I am calling it are found at (of all places) the 99Cent Only Stores, Dollar Tree, and some items (like the CAT Tourniquets and Condor Rip Away EMT Pouch) were bought at full retail elsewhere.

I will provide a break down of each item and their cost. I will include shipping in the cost of an item (if at all applicable). Tax is NOT factored in, because it would confuse the issue as tax rates vary radically within each state from city to city and county to county. Some items, like the CAT Tourniquet are optional.

Shall we begin?

Commercial IFAK:

Dimensions: 7" x 7.5 x 2.5"

IFAK Contents

1 - 4" Israeli Bandage or 4" ETD Dressing

2 - Pair of Nitrile Gloves

1 - H&H Compress Gauze (4.5" x 4yds)

1 - Asherman Chest Seal

1 - CAT Tourniquet

1 - Tape (1" x 10yds)

2 - 5" x 9" ABD Pads

1 - Nasopharyngeal Airway with Lubricant

1 - Decompression Needle

1 - EMT Shears

Cost: $150.00

Now for **my** PEAK or "Modified" IFAK:

Size: 8" H x 6" W x 3.5" D

1 Condor "Rip Away EMT Pouch" - $15.00

1 SOF Tourniquet (BLACK) - Generation II (optional) - $18.95

1 IDF Israeli Army Bandage - $5.97

1 EMT Shears - $4.50

1 non-sterile Triangular Bandage - $1.97

1 Pack Mole Skin - $6.50

1 Pack Quick Clot (mesh bag - 50 gram) - $13.50

3 rolls sterile gauze, 4 yards each - $1.00

2 "Ace" Style Bandages - $2.00

18 Alcohol Prep Pads - $0.50

4 count Picot Antacid Powder - $0.50

2 Bottles Murine "Real Tears" - $2.00

1 Tube Hydrocortizone Creme - $1.00

1 Tube Triple Antibiotic ointment - $1.00

2 rolls Kerlix 4 Yards - $2.00

16 count Halls Defense Vitamin C drops - $1.00

16 count Halls Honey Lemon Cough Drops - $1.00

Hand Sanitizer Spray - non alcohol - $1.00

Waterproof "silk" medical Tape - 1.5"x8 yards - $1.00

100 Assorted Curad Bandages - $3.00

Vaseline Lip Therapy - $1.00

Cold Gel Compression Wrap - $1.00

Instant Ice Pack - $1.00

Red Sharpie - $1.00

6 packs burn Gel - $4.80

6 count Tylenol travel packs - $1.00

6 count Alleve Tablets - $1.00

2 Pairs Blue Nitrile Gloves - $0.10

1 set metal tweezers - $1.00

1 Mylar Emergency Blanket - $1.00

1 Disposable CPR face Shield - $2.50

2 film canisters with assorted home medications (allergy pills, aspirin, etc.) - negligible cost.

Total including the optional Tourniquet: $98.79

Average Cost savings against top of the line commercial IFAKS? over $53.00

Assurance that *you* have built something that is not only good, but very much functional and serviceable, as well as know what is in your kit, backwards and forwards? Priceless.

All the details aside, anyone can customize this PEAK any way they see fit. NATO tourniquet instead of a CAT? Absolutely...it is *your* gear. My intention here is to show how one can be made fully custom by you for you, without breaking the bank.

Please note: medications, with a few exceptions, have been found to be effective well past their listed expiration dates.

Consider aspirin. Bayer AG puts two-year or three year dates on aspirin and says that it should be discarded after that. Chris Allen, a vice president at the Bayer unit that makes aspirin, says the dating is "pretty conservative"; when Bayer has tested four-year-old aspirin, it remained 100 percent effective, he says.

So why doesn't Bayer set a four-year expiration date? Because the company often changes packaging, and it undertakes "continuous improvement programs," Mr. Allen says. Each change triggers a need for more expiration-date testing, he says, and testing each time for a four-year life would be impractical.

Bayer has never tested aspirin beyond four years, Mr. Allen says. But Jens Carstensen has. Dr. Carstensen, professor emeritus at the University of Wisconsin's pharmacy school, who wrote what is considered the main text on drug stability, says, "I did a study of different aspirins, and after five years, Bayer was still excellent.

Aspirin, if made correctly, is very stable." Only one report known to the medical community linked an old drug to human toxicity. A 1963 Journal of the American Medical Association article said degraded tetracycline caused kidney damage. Even this study, though, has been challenged by other scientists. The Shelf Life program encountered no toxicity with tetracycline and typically found batches effective for more than two years beyond their   expiration   dates.

Chapter 9
Doomsday Preppers...Thoughts and

Reflections

Doomsday Preppers, the new "buzz" of "reality" based television programs. Focused on preppers, and their lifestyles. For me, it is a fun program to watch, but it is disconcerting at the same time. Let us take a look at the good, the bad, and the ugly.

The good:

It is fun to watch in the simplest sense, as it provides a basis of comparison, a good idea of what prepping involves, and some humor. Many of the people featured on the show have done quite a bit to be prepared.

One of the shortfalls of the program is the fact that each group or individual is forced by the show's producers to select only one scenario for which they are preparing. In my estimation, the more dramatic the scenario, the better.

I have seen some exceptionally good preparations and some exceptionally poor ones.

The preparations are reviewed and judged by a company headed by two very well known, and very "prep savvy" individuals on YouTube - SouthernPrepper1 and Engineer 775. I find these judgements to be solid and sound. The recommendations they give are exactly what I would have recommended to each group or individual.

The bad:

The downside to the show is the portrayal of these "preppers". While I understand each segment is edited for expedience, drama, and other basic principles of "reality" television, the editing leaves much to be desired. What do I mean? Each segment seems to be edited to marginalize the prepper community.

The producers seem to make each individual or group out to be "fringe" or even borderline crazy. This is, in my opinion, a way to make the preppers come across as "out of touch" with reality.

Especially when NatGeo displays *their* expert's opinion's on how likely the scenario that an individual or group is preparing for is going to happen. Some shows leave me shaking my head in wonder at the ignorance of not only the "experts", but of the general populace – the "sheeple" - as a whole.

While some scenarios, like the eruption of the Yellowstone super volcano, are very unlikely, things like economic collapse are staring us in the face. This leads me to the "ugly" part.

The ugly:

First and foremost, OPSEC. OPSEC - Operational Security - should be the first and foremost thing on every prepper's mind. You do *not* advertize your location, preparedness level, or even discuss them among mixed company. Why?

Simple. In a SHTF scenario, you will be a have. You will have food, water, shelter, fuel, security, and skills. Every other person, who are not prepping, will be a have not. What do you do when your neighbor, who knows you are prepared but is not prepared themselves, show up at your door begging for food, water, shelter, or protection?

When you turn them down, because of the finite nature of your preparations, what happens when the begging turns to desperation? You will have placed yourself in a very untenable situation that could result in violence, injury, or even death.

Your family is at risk. You are at risk. Everything you have becomes a driving force for the "have nots" to take from you to ensure their survival.

Every single person, or group featured on this show has compromised their basic OPSEC. Now a nation of "have nots" know who has food, water, and equipment. Some of those are likely to even be the neighbors of these preppers. Not wise in the least.

Secondly the so-called "experts" assessing the odds of something like economic collapse actually happening. These folks are sidelining and marginalizing the preppers featured simply by giving unrealistic and very untrue statistical analysis of many, if not most, of the scenarios.

Looking at history, and current events, one would reasonably be able to estimate the potential occurrence of economic collapse at much, much higher than .2%. This sidelining and marginalizing serves, in my opinion, only one function. To dissuade any person who has not yet started preparing from actually starting.

Preparing is so much more than being ready for economic collapse. It is insurance against catastrophe. How many people, who were unprepared or woefully under prepared, have had to rely on outside help to survive in a post disaster scenario?

Hundreds of thousands, if not millions, in the past century. Preparing keeps you out of 10 hour long lines waiting for a charity or government organization to hand out basic foodstuffs and water so you can make it another day or two.

It allows you to invest that time you have saved by being prepared in repair work, debris removal, contacting your insurance company, and securing your domicile. It also saves you from having to pay exorbitant or scalper-like pricing for items, like generators, ice, or fuel when you are in an extended disaster scenario, such as a recovery period after a major hurricane.

You must not base your thinking about prepping off of a television program. Just look at the nightly news and see how people are affected by massive natural disasters, and put yourself in their position.

Play the "what if" game. Look at your family, either immediate or extended, and think how will I care for, feed, and protect my loved ones if something really big happens. Being prepared is insurance. The odds of some disaster visiting you or your family are greater than .02%.

It is not imprudent to buy life insurance or homeowners insurance. Why not buy some survival insurance?

Got preps? Pray for the best, prepare for the worst.

ABOUT THE AUTHOR

Originally from Cutler Ridge, Florida (now called Cutler Bay), and one of the numerous people impacted by Hurricane Andrew, Don Pontious lives in Texas. Running his radio show and his various hobbies have commandeered a large portion of his spare time. He is the author of the blog Some Helpful Tips For Prepping, a Ham Radio Operator, and a general jack of all trades. He dreams of being a goat rancher, but he will always be a Ridge Rat.